The United States Of The World

*How the American government can guarantee economic
development and democratic freedoms worldwide.*

Daniel F. McNeill

Inter turbas et discordias pessimo cuique plurima vis, pax et quies bonis artibus indigent. Tacitus *Histories* Book IV I.

(In times of angry mobs and civil dissention, extreme power finds its way into the hands of the worst men; in times of peace and tranquility men skilled in the exercise of goodness are necessary.)

1

After the Civil War, historians began writing American history as though the domination of all Americans by the Federal Government was inevitable. Yet for a good part of our history the seat of the Federal Government, Washington D.C., did not exist and when it was created, it was not located in any of our states. We chose a separate location for it taking small portions of land from the states of Virginia and Maryland. Abraham Lincoln declared in his inaugural speech of March 4 1861 that the Federal Government was a "national" government yet it possessed no national territory except the District of Columbia which was a stateless district. The Constitution never uses the word "national" or "nation" or "Federal Government" anywhere. It says its purpose is to form "a more perfect union…for the united states of America" and it then enumerates powers that the executive, legislative and judicial branches of the new government possess. Even the limited powers assigned to Washington troubled Americans and they attached 10 amendments to the Constitution before ratifying it. The tenth amendment states: "The powers not delegated to the United States by the Constitution, nor prohibited by it to the States, are reserved to the States respectively, or to the people." Clearly the Constitution is about delegating certain powers to a central government and this would certainly have been an odd way to set up a "national" government since the powers delegated are limited. President Lincoln used the word "national" because his purpose was to make the Federal Government a national government. Historians accepted Lincoln's revolution and then it became necessary to explain in simple terms how Washington came to possess the revolutionary power that Lincoln's armies in the Civil War had won for it.

Historians used two concepts to help fashion their postwar version of our history, "America" and "the nation". "America" already existed before the first appearance on the east coast of European immigrants. "America" transformed Europeans soon after their arrival on her shores into Americans. The English colonists from England who arrived in 1620 at Plymouth in Massachusetts were some of the first Americans and the political compact they agreed to on their ship, the Mayflower, before settling on the land was an embryo of democratic concepts that would one day be embodied in the US Constitution that established Washington as the head of "the nation". Colonists in Massachusetts rebelled in 1689 for independent rule and, assembling an armed force of 1500 men, arrested the British governor Edmund Andros. This was the most important rebellion in "America" in early colonial times against British rule and was clearly, according to historians, the first rumblings of volcanic forces that would one day roar forth in a fiery blast and form "the nation". Massachusetts colonists fired their rifles at the British army at Lexington and Concord in 1775 and killed or wounded nearly 200 British soldiers as they drove the enemy regiments back to the safety of Boston. This allowed historians to again jump on the "America" bandwagon and announce that the Massachusetts men had revolted in "America" to set up an independent government for "the nation". According to historians, the Massachusetts men were American patriots and even before George Washington, a Virginian, came to Cambridge in 1775 to take command of their army, they had begun the American Revolution, the bold event that showed the world the deep strength seething within the American heart and soul to found "the nation". Samuel Adams, the organizer of the Massachusetts rebellion, instigated the Boston Tea Party, attended the first two continental congresses in Philadelphia, signed the Declaration of Independence, helped draft the Articles of Federation and supported the ratification of the Constitution by Massachusetts. Samuel Adams might have been elevated by historians to the level of an American hero like George Washington or Thomas Jefferson if he had not constantly and outspokenly made it clear to his fellow colonists that Massachusetts was his "country" and that he had led the rebellion against Britain in her name. We have records of him referring to Massachusetts as his "country" as far back as an essay he wrote on liberty and sedition in 1748 at a time when he could not possibly be referring to "the nation". In another essay in the Boston Gazette in 1771, he writes about "the liberties of our country". His "country", Massachusetts, had put an army in its fields, had issued its own flag and its own currency, the Pine Tree Shilling, and had fought alone for three months with an army of over 20,000 men against a powerful European nation. Adams left behind too much written evidence that proved that he was not rebelling in the name of "the nation" so historians ignored him as best they could and some even wrote books deriding him as a crank. No defined geographical area is named "America" and no nation has ever established itself, including within its borders a well-defined distinct people, on the North American continent. Samuel Adams might have admitted that he instigated the Massachusetts rebellion in "America" but he would never have admitted that he was an American patriot rather than a Massachusetts patriot or that he had rebelled against Britain in order to establish a nation with its seat in a place named The District of Columbia.

On June 16 1858 in Springfield Illinois, Abraham Lincoln gave his "House Divided" speech. The "house" was "the nation" but the word "house" better suited Lincoln's purpose. He wanted to put an end to "slavery agitation" but he complained that the Federal Government's Kansas-Nebraska Act had not ended but increased the agitation. "I believe," he said, "that this government cannot endure permanently half slave and half free. I do not expect the union to be dissolved. I do not expect the house to fall, but I do expect it will cease to be divided. It will become all one thing or all the other." Stephen Douglas, Lincoln's opponent in the election of 1858 for US Senator from Illinois, warned that Lincoln was calling for "a war of sections, a war of the North against the South, of the free states against the slave states." Seven years later more than 600,000 Americans from the north and the south had died fighting one another in 8000 fights including 384 major battles all over "America" but "the nation" survived whole and now free of slavery, although the man who had first proclaimed that a division existed in the union had been assassinated. There had certainly been political division over slavery but there had been no division at all in the "house" over the question of whether the 34 states of the union were sovereign or not. In 1861 all the states were sovereign but by 1865 state sovereignty with the power it had had before the Civil War was gone. How to rationalize the brutal tragic war that Lincoln's actions shortly after his inauguration as President on March 4 1861 had caused?

The rationalization was clear. It was a war to end slavery. Thousands and thousands of white men had maimed and killed one another in battles for four bloody years in order to free from their chains four million black African slaves. Nothing could be so false and yet so ready at hand for a simplistic explanation. It was red meat thrown into crowds of hungry historians eager to cheer for Lincoln's actions which had made the government in Washington D.C. supreme. Lincoln had warned in his "House Divided" speech that the "slavery agitation" in his opinion " will not cease until a crisis shall have been reached and past." He warned that "Either the opponents of slavery will arrest its further development...or its advocates will push it forward till it shall become itself lawful in all the states, old as well as new, north as well as south." He made a truthful judgment of the situation "the nation" faced. He was right that a crisis was coming. However he did not mention that the 34 states contending with one another over the issue of whether they should be free states or slave states were sovereign states and only they as sovereign states had the power to decide whether slavery should be legal or illegal in their states. The sovereignty of the states was itself the cause of the "slavery agitation." Lincoln did not mention that to stop the agitation and end the crisis something big had to be done against state sovereignty.

Looking back from the beginning of the twenty-first century, state sovereignty inspires few Americans and if you are bold enough to use the expression "states rights," you subject yourself to the ignominy of being associated with an old and outdated idea. But before the Civil War when Lincoln gave his "House Divided" speech state sovereignty was vibrantly alive and much more powerful than it is today. The Constitution granted the Federal Government exclusive sovereign power in military and diplomatic matters and this made it a national sovereign power only when dealing with foreign states. It also granted it powers over interstate commerce and interstate justice that were substantial but very far from a grant of full national sovereignty. President Madison wrote that the powers of the Federal Government "are few and defined" and that those left to state and local governments "are numerous and indefinite." It is implicit in the Constitution that every state is sovereign and that the sovereign powers granted Washington derived from the sovereign powers of the states. Put simply, the conundrum was that the Federal Government could not have obtained limited sovereign powers unless they had been obtained from some prior absolute sovereignty belonging to the states which the Constitution also limited. Looking back, it may appear a bitter thing that the states limited their sovereignty by granting bits of it to Washington by ratifying the Constitution. But the very opposite is true: the Constitution provided each state a real substantial workable sovereignty that was much more solid than absolute state sovereignty might have been. The reality was that none of the thirteen original colonies were capable, after freedom from British rule was won, of maintaining themselves as independent nations. The Constitution, granting exclusive military power to the Federal Government, gave each state a powerful sword and a huge shield against any potential predator state that might wish to invade them and take them over. Each state remained sovereign and by union with other states and the government in Washington D.C., each possessed a mighty army and navy to maintain each state's freedom. Let the Federal Government have exclusive power also over all diplomacy! States did not need, especially when their number had increased to 34 when Lincoln was inaugurated, the expense and effort of worldwide contacts with foreign states, some of whom had the might to subdue them and colonize them. The Constitution did not set up in Washington a government with full sovereignty and it granted each state a condition as close to local "national" sovereignty as was possible. At the time of Lincoln's "House Divided" speech, it was generally accepted north and south that Washington did not have the power under the Constitution to decide whether a state was a free state or a slave state. Only what was called "popular sovereignty" could decide the issue. The legal basis of slavery was state sovereignty. Steven Douglas said to Abraham Lincoln in their sixth debate on October 13 1858 in Quincy Illinois, "I hold that under the Constitution of the United States, each state of this union has the right to do as it please on the subject of slavery." Near the conclusion of his remarks, Douglas went on to state, "This republic can exist forever divided into free and slave states." Lincoln replied that he had no desire to argue with slavery in Kentucky or Virginia, but that Douglas would be happy to see slavery extend not just into the western territories but into the northern states. Lincoln's warning was valid because since states were sovereign, they could decide whether their state was slave or free. Slavery could be extended even to the northern states. State sovereignty with its extensive powers had to end if slavery was to end and only one government could gain power by using its power against both, that in Washington D.C.. However Lincoln did not mention in his debates with Douglas that the government in Washington alone possessed the power to further limit state sovereignty and end slavery. Lincoln bided his time.

Julius Caesar crossed the Rubicon River with his army, violated the sovereign authority of the Roman senate, made himself a dictator, created a new political basis for the Roman Empire, and assured the existence of the Roman Empire for 600 years under emperors with absolute power. The deification of Abraham Lincoln for the actions he took to start the Civil War and create a new America make the deification of Julius Caesar understandable. He killed a half million Gauls Julius Caesar and made war against whomever he wished for his own reasons, including against Romans. He had done too many unspeakable and atrocious things with superhuman cruelty to be remembered by historians as a mere mortal. He had to be deified to keep human eyes forever blind to his monstrous excesses. Deification too was necessary for Abraham Lincoln. Historians have labored for generations to portray each example of good behavior they can discover in his humdrum life before his election as president as one of many key moments of advancement towards moral and political greatness passed through by an uncouth uneducated Kentuckian born into a 16-by-18 foot log cabin. They portray his character as unflinchingly right-minded even though they all know he plotted behind the scenes like some Machiavellian renaissance prince to sandbag the state of Virginia and to force it to secede from the union so that he could invade it with a large army, annihilate its fighting men and rule over its citizens. Through all stages of his moral advancement he was an enemy of slavery. He lived until the age of seven in Kentucky with black slaves as natural to his surroundings as wilderness. His father and his illiterate mother moved from Kentucky, a slave state, to Indiana, a free state, and even in this picayune move cheer-leader historians have uncovered a fundamental moral commitment against slavery in the Lincoln nature that infected, they imagine, young Abraham. His astounding rise to the presidency in 1861 openly declaring his opposition to the extension of slavery to the states and territories west of the Mississippi River was rife with potential political and social tragedy. Abraham must have felt when Pinkerton detectives snuck him secretly into Washington for his inauguration to escape possible assassination that he was on a journey that no American had ever been on and that it must lead to a new America or else force "the nation" back to the moral darkness of the existence of slavery in some states enforced and legalized by state sovereignty. But escaping from Baltimore to the safety of Washington was just one of many anxious and ambiguous experiences on his revolutionary voyage that historians have refused to examine realistically. Abraham himself helped them by always keeping his real intentions as secret as possible. He was ready and willing even before he reached Washington to cross the Rubicon but unlike Caesar he was clever enough not to let anyone get a clear view, then or now, of his crossing.

Historians, in addition to their effort to create an imaginary comic-book picture of Abraham Lincoln's life and doings, also conveniently skip idealistically over what was at the heart of American experience during the period from the ratification of the Constitution in 1787 to the outbreak of Civil War in 1861. No one in "America" felt truly in their heart of hearts that a genuine political sentiment lived in them that united them to "the nation". Almost none of the signers of the Declaration of Independence and the creators of the Constitution had ever had the experience of living in a nation because they were colonists, not nationals of any nation. The successful rebellion and the creation of the union was certainly a thrilling emotional and political adventure but the vast majority of colonists lived in poverty and obscurity and many were indifferent to both events despite their magnificence. For the leaders of the Federal Government and the leaders of the united sovereign states that were the fruits of the adventure, the emotions of revolution faded and politicians were left with an extremely complicated federal-state political apparatus that was radical and difficult to use effectively because everything was new and untried and citizens were scattered over a huge territory living at the time of the Civil War under the laws of 34 distinct sovereign states. There was no good workable name for the new political structure because it was not one simple political structure such as makes up a nation. The New England novelist Nathaniel Hawthorne wrote about "the anomaly of two allegiances of which that of the State comes nearest home to a man's feelings, and includes the altar and the hearth, while the General Government claims his devotion only to an airy mode of law and has no symbol but a flag." Addressing national sentiment, he said, "I wonder that we Americans love our country at all, it having no oneness; and when you try to make it a matter of the heart, everything falls away except one's native state." Henry Thoreau wrote in his book *Walden,* "The majority of men lead lives of quiet desperation." In 1857 when the anti-slavery anti-federal-government radical, John Brown, came to Concord, Thoreau listened to his lecture against slavery and said that it was the first time in his life that he ever felt he belonged to a nation. Until he was 21 in 1830 Abraham Lincoln helped his father Thomas and his family by working for twenty-five cents a day clearing land, plowing fields, and building fences. He also worked daily on the farm his father had created in Indiana by chopping his way through a thick forest to clear a forty-acre homestead in a wilderness 600 miles from Washington. Washington at the time was inhabited sparsely. Young Abraham lived under governments in Indiana and in Washington D.C. but his skill he developed with an axe to earn money splitting rails, not nationalistic sentiment, was the weapon he used to free his spirit from the quiet desperation of his life in the wilderness. The high ends and the low ends of cultural experience of the period were rooted in the need to create new forms for political and religious and moral and intellectual awakenings that would provide an escape from individual barrenness and obscurity. Political speeches generated great popular enthusiasm and campaigns featured joyous parades that provided the means for flag waving and cheering. Politicians seeking federal-government positions argued over issues that were grand in scope but far removed from the daily plodding along of farm laborers and mechanics although the issues struck chords of interest in average people's hearts that did lift their experience for a while to a level beyond the ordinary. People scattered over a continent in small towns and lonely farms were open to experiences that their ordinary lot could not generate because little derives from nothingness and obscurity except more of the same. Abraham Lincoln was a champion of self-propulsion from the ordinary. With little education, he taught himself to read. He emigrated at 21 to Illinois and went patiently from rail-splitter to postman to land assayer to store owner and finally transcended his lot to a career as a lawyer. At the high end of cultural experience was New England Transcendentalism. Educated people in New England and elsewhere, frustrated by the lack of higher experience derived from their native circumstances, sought to enlarge their experience with anything gleaned from the past in European art, philosophy, religion and literature or from any higher experience at all available to them from worldwide cultural influences. They opened their souls to any experience that transcended their normal experience provided it was genuine. Politically, all over the north, Abolitionism was another source of escape from the ordinary. Nationalism was budding all over Europe providing inspiration for powerful nationalistic sentiments that were often substitutes for religious experience. In the United States, Abolitionism was partly a substitute for national feeling. When an Abolitionist spoke at a meeting with moral inspiration against the evils of slavery, he was speaking against a foul condition of human beings that was legal according the laws he lived under but outlawed by the laws of the nation that he so ardently desired might exist but in fact did not exist. Slaves were living means to escape the ordinary labor that enslaved most Americans. Slave owners existed in a realm nicely above the ordinary to the same degree that their slaves lived hopelessly below the ordinary painful lot of their fellow laboring humans. The Abolitionists flew off in their minds from the low immoral realms of slavery to the heavenly moral enthusiasms of antislavery agitation. For ordinary white farmers toiling in their fields, Transcendentalism took the form of agitation for "free soil". The new territories and states to the west of the Mississippi River offered the enticement of free land for impoverished whites. They feared that black slaves would also transcend the Mississippi and pollute the poor white man's Eldorado which was rooted not in gold but in free land. When Abraham Lincoln left his home in Springfield Illinois in February 1861 to be inaugurated president in Washington, he had transcended by his effort and intelligence the ordinary lot of most men in the western wilderness. He had referred many times in his speeches to "the nation" but he had never experienced genuinely what it feels like to live in a nation and he was about to start a war that he justified by a new revolutionary vision of the government he had been elected to in Washington.

The main theme of Lincoln's debates as the Republican candidate for senator in Illinois in 1858 against the Democrat Steven Douglas was his firm position against the extension of slavery to the new territories west of the Mississippi. He argued that the Federal Government had the power to restrict slavery in new states and territories. He was selected to run for president because he spoke eloquently in favor of this position which was a radical departure from the compromise doctrine, accepted by politicians north and south, that "popular sovereignty" in present and future states should determine whether slavery was legal or not. But before he was inaugurated on the March 4 1861, during the final months of James Buchanan's presidency, seven states in the deep south had seceded from the union and this meant that the issue Lincoln had campaigned on was no longer an issue. Seven slave states had seceded and thus had given up the rights they had possessed formerly as members of the union to deny that the Federal Government had the right to allow only free states in the new territories west of the Mississippi. Without yet being inaugurated President, Lincoln's issue had triumphed. Seven slave states had yielded to his position by seceding. The 34 states of the union had been reduced by seven to 27 but Lincoln and the Republican party had won the potential over time of a union of 41 states, of which only eight, Virginia, North Carolina, Arkansas, Tennessee, Kentucky, Maryland, Missouri and Delaware, were slave states. Lincoln did not have to start a war to save the union because he already had a union of 19 free states and 8 slave states with 14 new free states on the horizon. He also had an army of 35000 men that he could put into military action wherever necessary. Jefferson Davis, the president of the newly formed confederation of 7 seceded states, proclaimed he was ready for war if it came. Lincoln was ready too if it came. So why did Lincoln not let it come rather than cause it? For example, something would have had to be done about free passage for Union states down the Mississippi River past the seceded state of Mississippi and through the seceded state of Louisiana. For the present time, the 7 seceded states presented no problem for continued commerce among the states and if Jefferson Davis had dared to block commerce on the Mississippi, the union would have wholeheartedly backed President Lincoln and he would have had a just war instead of the unjust war that he decided to cause on April 6 1861.

At his inauguration on March 4, Lincoln had an opportunity to weaken slavery decisively in seceded states. A reasonable president would have seen that the support for southern slavery that even some northern politicians like Daniel Webster had consistently provided was now severely weakened. The seceded states had left the union and they had also left the Constitution's support for southern slavery. Lincoln himself had warned in his speeches that seceded states would give up the protection of the Constitution and of the Fugitive Slave Law which allowed them to pursue and capture escaped slaves in free states. If he were morally committed against slavery in new states and territories and was searching for a way like many Americans to end slavery in states where it was legal, why did he not proclaim in his inauguration address that slaves in seceded states were now free to escape across their state's borders to states loyal to the union and become free American citizens? If that angered 7 seceded states, so be it. He was now president of a union of 27 states with the power to crush easily the 7 seceded states if they started a war over any issue and Lincoln's fight in such a war would have been justified.

Lincoln appeared to have no reason to start a war. The seceded states had rashly broken their sworn allegiance to the Constitution and seceded without consulting their sister slave states. They were in grave danger. Florida was an easy target for predator European states. Taking it over would have been a minor operation for England or France. Texas could never have sustained on its own an invasion by Mexico. South Carolina and Georgia and other seceded slave states would have had to supply soldiers to aid Texas and this would have weakened them to the point of causing slave uprisings and wholesale slave escapes to the safety of states in Lincoln's union. Lincoln proclaimed in his inaugural address that he would not provoke war with the 7 seceded states and that only their action against the US could cause war. "In *your* hands," he said, "my dissatisfied fellow countrymen, and not in *mine*, is the momentous issue of civil war. The government will not assail *you*. You can have no conflict without being yourselves the aggressors.". He introduced the issue of war in his inauguration address, but he said nothing about using his power as president to not allow slavery west of the Mississippi nor did he mention the antislavery agitation in northern states which were the issues that had sparked his popularity with the antislavery Republican party and had made him president.

In his inaugural address, Lincoln introduced a radical new theme. He had carefully thought out his speech and written it out well before he reached Washington. He began his address and proceeded carefully exactly like a lawyer presenting a reasoned argument. He did not however, like the experienced lawyer that he was, reveal the specifics supporting his argument at the start. He first calmly proclaimed that no slave state had anything to fear from him regarding slavery. He said he would not interfere directly or indirectly with slavery in states where it already existed. He asserted that only states had the right to order and control their own domestic institutions, but this was far from asserting that every state was sovereign and, with a lawyer's skill in skirting issues, he avoided entirely in his speech any mention of state sovereignty. He asserted that he would enforce the Fugitive Slave Law and in speaking of the law, he mentioned that it could be enforced either by state or by national authority. After seven sentences reassuring all Americans that they need not fear any disruption of their peace and security from his administration, he again used the word "national". "It is seventy-two years since the first inauguration of a President under our national constitution." Here was at last the specifics of the case he was arguing: the Constitution was national, implying that the Constitution set up a nation. This was false because the Constitution set up not a nation, but "The government of the United States of America". It was false because a nation can not be constituted from several sovereign states but, false or not, an experienced and talented lawyer like Lincoln was out to win his case. He noted for the first time, referring indirectly to the seven seceded states, that there had been "a disruption in the union" and then quickly proceeded to justify his description of the Constitution as "national" by claiming that the union was perpetual. "I hold that, in contemplation of universal law, and of the Constitution, the Union of these states is perpetual". He related this assertion in his next sentence to his previous assertion that the Constitution was "national". "Perpetuity is implied, if not expressed, in the fundamental law of all national governments." Suddenly in Lincoln's mind "the nation" exists because a national constitution exists and a national government exists and they not only exist but they reinforce one another because the national constitution establishes a national government located in Washington D.C. that has its roots in a perpetual union. Instead of declaring again that there is a "house divided", Lincoln explains that there is now "a disruption in the union" but there is no disruption *of* the union because it is perpetual. A house now exists that can not be divided by anything at all, a house perpetual and undivided, a house in which Lincoln was living and of which he was the master.

Lincoln declares in his inaugural address nothing less than the sovereignty of the Federal Government. The Federal Government is no longer a *unum e pluribus*, a one from many. It is now a *unum contra plures,* a one against many. He was declaring that as president he had for four years sovereign authority over the states in the American union like a king. Surely he knew that George Washington, like the

ancient Roman general Cincinnatus, had left his army after its victory, refused to exercise sovereign power and retired to private life.
Certainly he knew that such a man, living in the old and sovereign
state of Virginia, would never have helped write the Constitution and
then served as the first president, if he knew that there was any chance
that he was creating a document that gave full sovereign authority to
a government that had no national territory and had as yet no location in a city to be given his name, Washington, and to be called
The District of Columbia. "The Union is perpetual," said Lincoln
in his address, "confirmed by the history of the Union itself. The
Union is much older than the Constitution. It was formed in fact,
by the Articles of Association in 1774. It was matured and continued
by the Declaration of Independence in 1776. It was further matured
and the faith of all the then thirteen States expressly plighted and
engaged that it should be perpetual, by the Articles of Confederation
in 1778." The full title of the Articles of Confederation is in fact
"Articles of Confederation and of Perpetual Union" but no mention
is made in the text itself of "perpetual union". Instead, in Article 3 it
is stated that "the said states hereby severally enter into a firm league
of friendship with one another..." The articles do not set up a nation
nor grant congress sovereign power. All sovereignty is retained by
the states. Lincoln says that the union established by the articles
had already existed in the Articles of Association in 1774 and it "was
matured and continued by the Declaration of Independence in 1776".
The Declaration did mature and continue a perpetual union but it
did so while also declaring "that these United Colonies are, and of
Right ought to be Free and Independent States..." Lincoln was right
that the union was perpetual but it was no longer the union continued by the Constitution if the Federal Government was fully sovereign. The perpetual union as Lincoln understood it had matured to
the radical point where it had no longer any need or use for "free and
independent states".

A perpetual union of sovereign states under the power of a national
government is a contradiction because separate sovereign states can
not synthesize and become a nation. You can have a union of sovereign

states or a nation but you can not have both. Only a perpetual union of subservient states can be a nation. Secession took place because the radical republicans threatened to use the Federal Government as a national government endowed with a degree of sovereignty that it had never had previously and that was not justified by the Constitution. Lincoln declared when he was leaving his home in Springfield and traveling to Washington for his inauguration as president that he was "an instrument of history." History was pushing him to go radically beyond the bits of sovereign power granted to him by the Constitution. The examples he cites in his inaugural address supporting perpetual union, the Articles of Association in 1774, the Declaration of Independence in 1776, and the Articles of Confederation in 1778, do not set up a nation or reduce the sovereignty of each of the united states. The Constitution does limit state sovereignty but the sovereignty that the central government is granted can operate with full power only when dealing with foreign states. The basis of perpetual union under the Constitution was perpetual state sovereignty and when the Federal Government with Lincoln elected president threatened to assume sovereignty over the American states, it broke the union.

Lincoln continued the revolutionary surge that was pushing himself and his fellow radical republicans forward to a new nation. In order to continue on to their new nation, he had to break the union even further. He had to cripple the sovereignty of all of the states and force on all Americans a union of states without their former sovereignty. Already on March 5, the day after his inauguration as president, a means was presented to him to start a war against the 7 seceded states. Robert Anderson, the commander of Fort Sumter, a fort in the harbor of South Carolina, a seceded state, wrote that he had enough supplies to last only six weeks. If Lincoln sent ships to supply and defend the federal fort, which was his right under the Constitution, it might start a war and also push four slave states of the upper South, including Virginia which had a border with Washington D.C., to secede. General Winfield Scott, the head of the army, strongly advised Lincoln to abandon the fort. Scott told Lincoln that to control it would require a fleet of war vessels, five thousand regular troops plus twenty thousand volunteers. Scott's final sentence in the letter he wrote Lincoln about the matter read, "To raise, organize and discipline such an army, would require new acts of Congress and from six to eight months." On March 18, at a meeting of his cabinet, Lincoln asked its members to vote on whether or not to supply and defend the fort. His Secretary of State, William Seward, told Lincoln it would provoke war and voted no. Four other members voted no. The idea was defeated 5 to 2 but Lincoln now possessed an option ready at hand to start his war. By the end of March, Lincoln ordered his new Secretary of War, Simon Cameron, to draw up plans for the relief of the fort. By this time, some of his advisors had warned Lincoln that states had too much power and the actions he took against them prove that he agreed.

On the first of April 1861, the outbreak of the Civil War was just 15 days away. President Lincoln could look out the windows of the White House across the Potomac River at the green fields of Virginia. He confessed about this time just a few days before the bombardment by South Carolina of Fort Sumter that, "All the troubles and anxieties of his life had not equaled those which intervened between this time and the fall of Fort Sumter." Despite his anxieties, as he thought of the possibility of war, he must have thought also about the best place for it to be fought. Historians always rush by these decisive days at the beginning of April and cover their rush forward with general statements about how Washington and Lincoln were in grave danger from secessionist war hawks in the south. They skip quickly by the reasons why four more southern states seceded from the union during these days and shortly afterwards and swelled the ranks of the secessionists from 7 to 11 states. Washington was in no danger at all of attack during these early days of April from the south through the state of Virginia. Virginia was in danger from an attack from Washington reinforced by northern troops and when Lincoln succeeded by his actions to force Virginians to secede, Virginia was in grave alarming danger. In a proclamation after the bombardment of Fort Sumter on April 12 of April 15, Lincoln demanded that all loyal states provide him with troops to help make up an army of 75,000 men. A convention in session in Richmond Virginia debating the question of secession from the union had sent a commission to Washington to meet with Lincoln to try to get assurances that they were in no danger of being attacked. They met with Lincoln on April 13 but he said nothing to them about the proclamation of April 15 that he was about to issue demanding that all loyal states furnish his government with75,000 men to help him attack the 7 seceded states. One member of the commission, Mr. William Scott, was shocked when he returned to Richmond and learned there of Lincoln's proclamation. "I must confess", said Mr. Scott, "that I was so entirely taken by surprise by the appearance of the proclamation, that I did not for a moment believe that it was authentic. I believed that it was a sensation document, gotten up by some mischievous persons;". "Like my colleagues," Mr. Scott said in conclusion, "I therefore think, in view of this communication of the President to the Convention, through this Committee, and in view of the proclamation of the President of the United States to the whole people, that there is no hope of an amicable arrangement with the Administration. I have cherished, sir, a most ardent hope that matters would be solved peaceably. If there be any man upon this floor who has cherished a more ardent, a more decided, a more, I must say, religious and sincere love for this Union than any other, I claim to be that man... I must confess that my hopes in the perpetuation of the Union, as it now stands, have been greatly weakened, if they have not been entirely destroyed." He was aware as were others at the convention that the fervor for war in the northern states after the bombardment of Fort Sumter had gone beyond all possible restraint. Even so, William Scott still argued for Virginia not to secede from the union. Virginia would be in grave frightful danger. "What is our state of preparation?" asked Mr. Scott. "Where is our ordnance? Where is our musketry? Where are our rifles? Where, in fact, are any of the munitions of war, which are indispensable for our security? Sir, you may talk about courage, and you may talk about chivalry; but I say it is not true courage and true chivalry to rush into such an unequal contest as that. I say, in my judgment it would be folly and fool-hardiness in the extreme." Then he went on about the frightful danger of where the war would be fought if Virginia were to secede. It would not be fought in the swamps of South Carolina or in Florida with its fierce heat. "Here is a war waging," he said. "Here is an immense preparation made on the part of the

United States Government for carrying on that war. The present seat of that war is at a remote part of the Union. It is now confined to the region about the city of Charleston and the city of Pensacola. These are the points where the war is now seated. What would be the effect of the immediate secession of Virginia? It would be to transfer the seat of war from the Gulf of Mexico, and from the extreme Southern part of our Atlantic coast, to the bosom of Virginia. Yes, sir, your county [Loudoun] that county situated upon the old highway, North and South; the county of Jefferson and the county of Berkeley, would be the Flanders in this war. I could not conceive of any greater favor that you could confer upon this Black Republican administration than to secede now. By Virginia's seceding you transfer the seat of war to this fertile and salubrious country. You transfer it to a country that furnishes every supply that is necessary for the support of the troops; to a climate that is entirely salubrious to the Northern troops who would be engaged in prosecuting the war. Yes, sir, you bring it home to your own fair cities and families. You go into this war without any aid from any quarter. We have no alliance with the Confederate States, nor our sister border States not yet seceded, and Virginia would stand alone between the Federal Government and the Confederate States of the South. She would be the battle ground."

Virginia had no reason to secede from the union and attack Washington D.C.. Lincoln had a reason for forcing Virginia out of the union. The convention had begun in Richmond on February 13 to debate the question of secession. Virginians had been acting since then in their daily debates in a democratic manner as citizens loyal to the union and members of a sovereign state. Lincoln, Washington, Americans and the world had been listening to their daily debates about the positive and negative aspects of seceding from the union. In Maryland to the north of Washington, a slave state like Virginia, slave owners and secessionists had rioted against federal authority. Lincoln had jailed men using his military and suspended the right of habeas corpus. Using the Pinkerton detective agency, he had set up a federal police network to spy on and arrest citizens who disagreed with his policies. He was jailing anyone he pleased in Maryland for speaking in favor of secession and here before him across the fields of Virginia 106 miles away in Richmond, 3 hours away by train, the political and moral leaders of Virginia were discussing secession daily just as though as citizens of a sovereign state they had the right to secede from the union and could vote for secession any day they wished. In Lincoln's eyes, since they assumed they had the right to vote for secession, they were acting as citizens of a sovereign state. He endured with great difficulty the free and open democratic deliberations going on in Virginia. The Virginians were asserting the same sovereign rights as members of the union that seven states had asserted by voting to secede from the union. Lincoln had his response to South Carolina's secession ready. He had his ships ready to sail to Charleston and force their way into Charleston harbor to the aid of Fort Sumter. He had a loaded gun that he was ready to send to South Carolina so that authorities there could fire it and start the Civil War. He had his chance to strike a blow to establish his government's sovereignty. But he waited. He hesitated. Then at the height of the "crisis" over Fort Sumter that historians have invented and did not exist, the Virginian men at their convention in Richmond on April 4 decided to vote on whether or not to secede from the Union. They voted 88 votes to 44 not to secede. The "crisis" was over. Washington D.C. had nothing to fear from the most powerful state in the south. War was no longer possible in the green salubrious fields of Virginia that Lincoln could see across the Potomac River from the White House. His hesitation was suddenly gone. He acted decisively. But he did more than just order ships to sail to Fort Sumter in Charleston harbor because he had to be sure that they started the war. On April 6, two days after the Virginians had voted not to secede, he sent a courier, Robert S. Chew, to inform the governor of South Carolina, Andrew W. Pickins, that he was sending ships to supply Fort Sumter and that if they were resisted, he would supply the fort with men, arms and munitions. On April 9, 5 days after Virginians had voted not to secede, Lincoln's fleet of ships was off with its destination Fort Sumter. On April 12, South Carolina forces bombarded the fort and it surrendered on April 13, nine days after Virginians had voted not to secede. On April 15, Lincoln, without the approval of Congress which was not in session, issued the proclamation demanding that all states loyal to the union, including of course Virginia, supply the government in Washington with 75,000 volunteers for the war against the 7 seceded states. The governor of Virginia, John Letcher, immediately replied to Simon Cameron, Lincoln's Secretary of War, who had telegraphed him on April 15 requesting troops, that Virginia would not supply them. "Your object", wrote governor Letcher, "is to subjugate the Southern States, and a requisition made upon me for such an object - an object, in my judgment, not within the purview of the Constitution or the act of 1795 - will not be complied with. You have chosen to inaugurate civil war, and, having done so, we will meet it in a spirit as determined as the administration has exhibited toward the South." On April 17, 13 days after Virginians had voted in convention not to secede from the union, they again voted on the issue and voted by a vote of 85 to 45 to secede. On May 1 Lincoln wrote in a letter to Gustave Fox, the commander of the ships he had sent to supply Fort Sumter, "You and I both antici-pated that the cause of the country would be advanced by making the attempt of provision Fort Sumter, even if it should fail; and it is no small consolation now to feel that our anticipation is justified by the result." Ten weeks after the bombardment of the fort, Lincoln confessed to his friend Orville Browning, "The plan succeeded. They attacked Sumter- it fell and thus did more service than it otherwise could." On April 18, the day after Virginians voted to secede, a member of the convention, Mr. R. Y. Conrad of Frederick, Virginia, voiced his reaction to the events that Lincoln had set in motion on April 6 to start the war. Mr. Conrad said, "I deem this the best and the safest position which Virginia can assume at this time-to resist the President of the United States and the Federal authorities upon the ground that they are exercising or attempt-ing to exercise usurped power over the people of this Commonwealth and the people of other States in this Union; and to hold them respon-sible as individuals, as lawless usurpers of power, and not acting under the Constitution of the Federal Government or any other Constitution; and I think, sir, that it is due to the people of Virginia; it is due to the safety of the people of Virginia; it is due to ourselves in some mode or other, to declare to the world that we have not chosen, by a mere volun-tary act, to overturn this Federal Government, which I admit that the people of Virginia had a right to do under the circumstances. That we did not, upon a mere act of volition, destroy the integrity of this Union; but that we did it upon the ground that this Federal authority, elected temporarily under the Constitution, holding office for a short term, had undertaken to disregard all constitutional limitation, and, in violation of the Constitution and of the natural rights of the people of Virginia and of the United States, are attempting to exercise lawless, usurped authority". On May 23 the question of secession from the union was voted on by the whole people of Virginia. They voted for secession by a vote of 132,201 to 37,451.

Lincoln had admitted to the three commissioners from Virginia who met with him on April 13 in Washington before his proclamation of April 15 that began the war that he had read the proceedings of the convention in Richmond. He knew therefore that Virginians at the convention had voted on April 4 not to secede from the union. He was sure that he faced no danger from Virginia and then two days later he sent a letter by his courier, Robert S. Chew, to the governor of South Carolina, Mr. Pichens, informing him that he was sending ships to reinforce Fort Sumter. He provoked the attack on the fort two days after finding out that Virginians had voted not to secede from the union. On July 21 a federal army of 30,000 men from the northern states commanded by a general appointed by Lincoln crossed the Potomac River and invaded Virginia, the home state of Thomas Jefferson and George Washington.

2

The whole continent of North America had no nation anywhere when the first European colonists arrived in the sixteenth century. The general disposition of humanity throughout recorded history has been the tribe at the lower end and the empire at the high end with nations scattered in between very rarely. The Europeans met no nation in North America and this made subjection of the natives and colonization easy. The Spanish conquerors of Mexico met an empire with a central government in Mexico City but some conquered tribes eagerly aided the Spaniards crush the empire. States developed in North America as they had in Africa during the nineteenth century. European nations conquered the natives and outlined on maps the boundaries of their colonies. The colonies then became states when the Europeans departed. The states in Africa are now nations enclosed within frontiers established by Europeans. In North America, the Europeans left behind colonies that became at their departure provinces or states but not nations.

The nation-state is a European invention. The Romans began the long fight to establish their empire beginning as a tribe living among the 7 hills of Rome. European nations developed typically in patterns of historical experiences much like those of the Romans, but the Romans ended up with an empire, the Europeans with the nation-state. The Romans fought heroic battles to enlarge their territory. They subdued neighboring tribes and established new borders and then went beyond the borders to new conquests. So did Europeans. The Romans made a central city, Rome, the seat of their expanded territory. The Europeans did the same setting up London and Paris, Madrid and Lisbon and other European cities as the seat of some expanded territory. The Romans took their tribal language, Latin, refined it and forced it on the natives of their conquered territories. The English, French, Spanish, Portuguese and all the other leading tribes of other European areas did the same. The most powerful confederation of tribes selected one of many languages, refined it and forced it on all the remaining tribes in their nation-state. The Romans won heroic life and death struggles with enemies to confirm their conquests and their imperial identity as Romans in a settled territory with a distinct language. The Europeans did the same except that they called their newly founded empires states. The European states grew up over long periods of crises and wars into firmly established units of peoples with well developed languages protected by armies eager for glorious wars to vindicate their national honor. The African and American states never went through similar experiences. Europeans left them with the boundaries of states and with European languages but without a common creative and dramatic historical experience necessary to give birth to a nation.

It was a good thing that the American states did not become nation-states as in Europe, a blessing. Already in the eighteenth century, the most powerful European states were growing rich from the slave trade and establishing slave colonies on the Caribbean islands to the south of the American states to produce sugar and reap huge profits by the brutal inhuman work schedules they inflicted on African slaves. All the American states north and south also exploited the labor of African slaves and their ships made profits from the slave trade that later provided capital to revolutionize manufacturing in the north using advanced technologies. The American rebellion against the British nation-state began in the northeast in New England and could have failed if it had not been joined by Virginia and other slave colonies partly to assure for themselves the continuation of slavery. When freed from Britain, none of the

13 new American states were strong enough to become nation-states and they needed union with one another to protect themselves from warlike European states always poised for war with one another or else out on the seas searching for territories to conquer and exploit. The British were the most successful colonizers. Even after yielding freedom to the thirteen American states situated along the Atlantic coast, they still possessed Canada with a territory many times larger than the territory of the American states. The British conquest and pacification of India permitted the largesse of outlawing slavery in the British Empire in 1833. The cost of labor in India was so low it made slavery in comparison too costly. By that time, slavery had petered out in America in the northern states and the outlawing of slavery in the British Empire made the break the southern slave states had made with Britain in the American rebellion fortunate. It was a blessing that the American states were not forced to rely only on their own military for protection. This prevented them from seeking colonies around the world and because they were unified by the Federal Government in Washington, when the peoples of the 13 states emigrated westward, instead of setting up colonies like the Europeans, they set up independent sovereign states with settled borders and democratic institutions of self-government and joined them to their perpetual union.

Washington D.C. was created in 1790 for the purpose of governing the union of states with strictly limited power and also to protect the union. The site along the Potomac river was selected by George Washington himself from sections of land from the states of Virginia and Maryland. The new city in a stateless location was named Washington and George Washington the man was the first president of the new government of the united states established by the ratification of the Constitution by the thirteen original states. Before ratification, the government set up by the Articles of Confederation was simply unable to govern and the thirteen states all went their own way as was their right as sovereign states. They refused to pay taxes to the central government which operated without any real authority and was disrespected by foreign states. The government in Washington established by the Constitution had full authority to deal with foreign states and some power of taxation but its influence over its own states was marginal and at its beginnings mostly irrelevant. However its authority, although partial, was real and set up legally in a Constitution. The judicial authority established by the Constitution provided for circuit federal courts to travel through the thirteen states with the power to review and reject the decisions of state courts. The Federal Government since its beginning, although with marginal authority, nonetheless seized and used every power it possessed to give itself more power. At the top of the federal circuit courts was the Supreme Court. It asserted almost immediately its right to declare unconstitutional laws of both the states and the Federal Government. The Constitution was the supposed guide to its decisions which were supposedly to be based on a regard for the powers expressly granted the Federal Government and written down in the Constitution. In 1803, in the case Marbury vs. Madison, the Supreme Court ruled that the Federal Government had not only expressed powers but implied powers. The decision opened up for use legal powers beyond what was granted in the Constitution and gave the Supreme Court itself expanded power. Historians eager to push the beginnings of "the nation" well back in time even before the ratification of the Constitution refuse to criticize power-grabbing by decisions of the Supreme Court. Powers added to Washington are always viewed as natural and necessary since historians argue that the union was a nation from the beginning and not merely a union of sovereign states. According to them, the infant nation required only Abraham Lincoln's extraordinary acts of political opportunism to bud forth gloriously as an adult and manly nation. In reality, the power-grabbing by the Supreme Court and presidents and congresses should have led keen and truthful historians to the simple realization that Washington was not given originally enough powers to act within the union like the central governments of nation-states. The Supreme Court grabbed more power when it could because it was not given much by the Constitution. Abraham Lincoln grabbed power by starting a war using his power as head of the military granted him by the Constitution, but it was an illegal war because the Constitution certainly did not grant him an implied power to use his army and navy in an all-out war against his own people.

The union of the thirteen original states was constituted uniquely. The Constitution is generally understood to have been a masterful creation using doctrines of revolutionary European political theorists of the age of enlightenment. This is only partly true. Rationalist philosophers in Europe railed against all the stupidities they encountered including the endless wars among their European nation-states but none of them theorized about setting up some kind of new supranational government whose purpose and being was designed to unite states rather than to be only just another national state among national states. The government of the United States of America was just such a supranational creation. The government in Washington set up by the Constitution was "The Government *of* the United States". It had a purpose and a being *for* the united states not *over* the united states. Most likely few Americans in 1787 understood the new government. The best way to describe it to them would have been to assert that Washington, located in no state, was the seat of a government of an international union of nations and that if the thirteen states acted as nations with limited sovereignty and if Washington acted as a government with its sovereign authority restricted even more than state authority, the unique new political apparatus would work well and profit all Americans.

One head of a government in Europe in 1803 was already working towards a new revolutionary union of states. Napoleon's army had already subdued enough nation-states and empires to be well on his way towards a united states of Europe. He was preparing to invade Britain to join it by force into his empire dominated by Paris. Meanwhile, he did more to create the United States of America as the union stood at the time of Abraham Lincoln's presidency and as it stands today than anyone else. He sold the territory France possessed west of the Mississippi River, from Louisiana on the gulf of Mexico to territory in the far northwest on the Pacific Ocean including territories today part of Canada, enough territory to create 14 new American states, to President Thomas Jefferson for 3 cents an acre. Napoleon failed to create a United States in Europe but he expanded the territory of the United States already existing in America on the east coast of the Atlantic extending west to the Mississippi River to twice its size.

President Jefferson was disturbed when he thought of what consequences for the American political system were sure to follow from the Louisiana Purchase. Settlers from the thirteen states of the union were already moving westward into lands east of the Mississippi to the west of the 13 states. New states of the union were being formed and their addition was already changing the nature of the union. Before, while there were just 13 states along the Atlantic coast, the Federal Government of the union was felt to be solidly in the control of leading men of the 13 states. Each state legislature voted for two men, selected from the upper educated classes, to the federal Senate in Washington composed of only 26 men. Almost all of them were Protestants of Anglo-Saxon origin. They had real power to advise the president and could vote to either block or approve foreign treaties which he was obligated to propose to them for their vote. At this time, the Federal Government was like a gentleman's political club easily within the reach of rich men who met together periodically in Washington with their fellow English-speaking countrymen from various states ready to handle both political and economic business for their mutual profit. The incredible astonishing union of 50 democratic sovereign states that developed from this initial union, small and modest in comparison to its later size, can not be described adequately with one or two words like "America" or "the nation". Was the union of the original thirteen colonies a nation? It was close to being one. The European counterparts of the rich middle-class men who met as officers in Washington assembled in Europe to create and rule nation-states. The nation-states in Europe were created by middle-class lawyers, allied if necessary with the nobility, to assure by law their class's riches and exempt the rich from paying taxes on their wealth. In America, it was the union of states that guaranteed the position of rich men by reinforcing their state laws with federal laws. Napoleon was doing his best with his army to exile from power the nobility in his empire and to set up in Europe in united states the rule of the middle class universally. He was trying to create the basis for some future federal structure in Europe that already existed in America and he helped double the size of the American union by the Louisiana Purchase. The original American union did function something like a nation. Men from the thirteen states had given up for their states a national army, but they could maintain state militias and have a career in their American army. They gave up diplomacy but they could become American diplomats. All types of federal judicial and bureaucratic appointments were available as supplements to state offices of the same type. But the sense of being in control of Washington's doings started slipping away from men in states along the Atlantic coast as settlers moved to the west towards the Mississippi River. The Federal Government supported in the new territories land speculators and slave owners eager to drive Indians from their lands and to use the new territories for slave plantations. The nation-states of England, France, and Spain had also treated native Americans cruelly but their national honor at least sewed a few threads of moral fiber in their colonial administrators that lessened somewhat their harsh rule. The new American "nation" had no moral fiber when dealing with native Americans. Settlers stole their lands and forcibly relocated them on the plains to the west of the Mississippi. The Indian Wars were one of two early sources of anti-national sentiment. Some people questioned what type of "nation" they were a part of that could treat native Americans so cruelly and steal their lands. Under President Van Buren, a treaty had been approved with the Cherokees which amounted to nothing less than their forced removal from their land in Georgia to the plains west of the Mississippi. In April 1838 Ralph Waldo Emerson wrote an open letter to the President questioning "the nation". "...a crime is projected that confounds our understandings by its magnitude, a crime that really deprives us as well as the Cherokees of a country for how could we call the conspiracy that should crush these poor Indians our government, or the land that was cursed by their parting and dying imprecations our country anymore?" The union made its way all the way to California and the Pacific Ocean and later out of North America to the state of Hawaii in the middle of the Pacific, but did "the nation" make its way too along with the union? The other source of early disunion was the War of 1812 with England. Opposed to the war, the four states of the New England area held a convention in Hartford Connecticut to consider secession from the union.

Power in Washington was used from the beginning mainly at the universal level. It has always been a problem to understand what Washington does or is supposed to do because almost all governmental business in the united states was and is done in the states by state governments. Washington maintains an army and navy, a diplomatic service and a federal judicial system. It provides a postal system and forts in harbors to regulate shipping and customs and other general services, but it was never given direct control of the most important functions governing the daily lives of Americans. The states build roads and provide police and courts and handle almost all important functions such as control of education and hospitals and banks. However, Washington's power at the universal level was grand at its beginning and its future potential was enormous. Benjamin Franklin was the first to understand and use American power at the universal level. Born in Boston in 1706, he ran away from his family to Philadelphia, made money running a newspaper and in 1757, now an accomplished figure of The Enlightenment, he jumped from concrete activities in America to a more universal function by traveling to London as a representative of the colony of Pennsylvania in its petitions to the British government about the control of the colony. Franklin, a loyal British citizen, remained in London until 1775. By then he was the colonial representative also of Georgia, New Jersey and Massachusetts and he had begun working actively for American independence at the international level. He was elected to the Second Continental Congress, signed the Declaration of Independence, became the Ambassador to France, and signed the Treaty of Alliance with Louis XVI which secured for the American rebels loans and French military support crucial for the victory at Yorktown in Virginia which secured American independence. He was an outstanding revolutionary at the universal level. He was a delegate to the Constitutional Convention and signed the Constitution. All his actions proved that "America" could never count politically unless it had the unassailable sovereign power to act as an equal among nation-states at the universal and international level. The best the Washington government could do at this level when it was 25 years old in 1812 was go to war with England. It had the power to wage war and it used it first in wars against native Indian tribes and then against the British Empire. Americans succeeded in burning down York, a city in Canada that later was named Toronto. The English in turn burned down the city of Washington. Washington rose from its ashes and again proved in 1846 that it was established to accomplish at least some things at the concrete and practical level by invading Mexico.

Few in the states had complained when Washington, again strutting its power on the international stage, bullied Spain into ceding to it the territory of Florida but the Mexican war aroused deep anti-union sentiment. Henry Thoreau refused to pay a local tax as a protest against Washington's new war and went to jail. Thoreau acted concretely against the war power ceded absolutely to the Federal Government. In 1859 Thoreau wrote in his great essay *Civil Disobedience*, "I heartily accept the motto, 'That government is best which governs least;' and I should like to see it acted up to more rapidly and systematically. Carried out, it finally amounts to this, which also I believe--'That government is best which governs not at all;' " Not only did many Americans protest against the war, but a question was subsumed by the new unjustified war: where was "America" located? How did it happen that "America" with 13 states could be "America" with Vermont, the fourteenth state, added? Now in 1846 President Polk was invading Mexico to grab Texas from Mexico for the union, so where was "America"? Could it be in Texas too? By 1846, 16 new states had been admitted to the union and they were already new parts of "America" but Texas had been part of Mexico and it was 1900 miles from Thoreau in Concord Massachusetts in his jail. Abraham Lincoln was a member of Congress in Washington in 1847. He also like Henry Thoreau and many others opposed the war because it was an unjustified use of the federal war power. Lincoln's moral stand against the war hurt his popularity among voters in his home state of Illinois. Most citizens of Illinois cheered wholeheartedly for the war. Most likely it taught Lincoln that many Americans favored war and did not care whom their wars were against or who started them.

The real central moral purpose of the new government of the union established by the Constitution was for the central government neither to start wars using its war and diplomacy powers, nor to cancel state laws using its judicial power and to meddle in states' economies with Congress's commerce power. Its duty was to obey the truly sacred command laid upon Washington in the Constitution in Article IV section 4: "The United States shall guarantee to every State in this Union a Republican Form of Government, and shall protect each of them against Invasion..." This command should be forever shouted into the ear of every federal politician interested only in expanding federal power and equally into the ear of every historian taking the high and facile road to intellectual importance by forever searching for "the nation". Peace within each state is the nation. A democratic government in each state free to make its own laws and free to govern its own business is the nation. Freedom from invasion by all enemies, foreign and domestic, is the nation. America is nowhere because its shape should be forever protean always changing to accommodate itself to living forms embodying the democratic acts of sovereign states necessary for vital political and personal freedoms. America exists anywhere in any of our 50 states whenever an American citizen from any racial origin and from any location anywhere in the world decides to exercise the extraordinary American right unknown anywhere else to live and to work and to become a free citizen of any state of our 50 sovereign states with the right to vote and stand for election to offices in his chosen democratic state merely by residing in it.

The Federal Government was pledged before the Civil War to support democracy in independent states and to share sovereign powers with them for the union's mutual benefit. The parade of new states went on and on and on. Vermont in 1791, Kentucky in 1792, Tennessee 1796, Ohio 1803, Louisiana 1812, Indiana 1816, Mississippi 1816, Illinois 1818, Alabama 1819, Maine 1820, Missouri 1821, Arkansas 1836, Michigan 1837, Florida 1845, Texas 1845, Iowa 1846, Wisconsin 1848, California 1850, Minnesota 1858, Oregon 1859, Kansas 1861. The federal senate filled to 68 members, the House of Representatives swelled. Could such a union of states from Maine on the Atlantic Ocean to California 3000 miles away on the Pacific Ocean realistically be construed as *a* nation? In 1858 when Lincoln declared that the "house" was "divided", there were 32 states in the house. Three years later, two more states joined the union. He was obliged as all presidents to obey the command of Article IV section 4 of the Constitution to "guarantee to every State in this Union a Republican Form of Government". After his inauguration, he took away the right of habeas corpus and put the state of Maryland under martial law. He was also obligated with respect to states, according to the oath he took to protect and defend the Constitution, to "protect each of them against Invasion;..." When his first invasion of the state of Virginia failed in July 1861, he patiently built up his navy and army and invaded Virginia again in March 1862, this time not with 30,000 men but with 120,000. Virginians held their breath and waited to defend themselves with at most 85,000 men.

3

The Civil War was a life or death struggle between a fully sovereign state, Virginia, that had not wanted to be fully sovereign, and a non-state, the Federal Government, that was prohibited by the spirit and the letter of the Constitution from acting as a fully sovereign state against American states but did so anyway. Such a war between men assembling in Washington D.C. from all the northern states and those assembling in Virginia from seceded states could not have happened unless it had been devised by political machinations. Extremists in the northern and southern states had long been howling for war but it was strategically impossible to put a war actually in operation because America was composed everywhere of sovereign states with borders just like nation-states but without the right to declare war on anyone. Each state had a militia, a small military necessary in case of outbreaks of public disorder, but they had no armies or any need for armies. Washington alone had an army of about 35,000 men. If a state were crazy enough to expand its militia in order to go to war with another American state, Washington would immediately use its army to prevent it for the public good. If a state were nonetheless insane enough to take its militia beyond its borders, it could only realistically accomplish this if its goal was war with a neighboring state. Otherwise, it would have had to have permission from a neighboring state to pass through it and perhaps have needed permission from other states to reach the enemy American state that it planned to invade. One reason for assigning all power to make war to the Federal Government was to avoid and make impossible wars between the states. At the time of Lincoln's journey to Washington to be inaugurated in March 1861, seven states had seceded. Historians, looking back at the situation, have been overly eager to portray Lincoln and Washington as being in grave danger because the seven seceded states were talking war and assembling some forces. There were riots in Baltimore against a Massachusetts regiment coming to Washington to defend the president that caused some deaths and there were other displays of tensions. But Washington D.C. was not threatened by invasion. Virginia and the state to its immediate south, North Carolina, had not seceded and Virginia was opposed to secession. An army from South Carolina, a seceded state, would have had to cross through North Carolina and Virginia with a supply column stretching back 500 miles to invade Washington. Lincoln was in no danger. In fact, even after his proclamation of war on April 15, his wife Mary, after discovering funds available to her to decorate the upper floors of the White House, went on a shopping spree in May for furnishings to Philadelphia and New York, the first of eleven buying trips she would make during the war. Lincoln waited until July to send a 30,000 man force under General McDowell into Virginia. Even its defeat was easy enough for Lincoln to endure because the northern states were so stunned that they eagerly sent thousands and thousands of young men to Washington to train for another invasion of Virginia. Virginia, which had ceded power to Washington to raise a federal army by ratifying the Constitution, was now forced by Washington to raise its own army. Lincoln and Washington waited leisurely 8 months before the next invasion. Mary Lincoln held a reception in the White House for 500 guests. When Lincoln's large army was at last ready to go south, the political leaders in Virginia panicked. They decided at a meeting to abandon Richmond. Robert E. Lee was present at the meeting. He told them that they must defend Richmond. General Lee, who later defeated Lincoln's armies four times on Virginian soil, did not want to fight any American anywhere but his honor as a soldier and as a man and Lincoln's machinations left him no choice but to use his sword, as long as he had the physical means to fight, to defend every man woman and child in Virginia from harm.

Virginia was a sovereign state under the union and with the union broken it was natural and unproblematic for it to act with full sovereignty. Lincoln and Washington however began the war with extremely limited sovereignty and usurping more sovereignty or acting with full sovereignty was problematic. When Napoleon made his *coup d'etat*, he was the head of the army and he took control of a government that was already set up to rule as a fully sovereign government of a state. Cromwell as a dictator in England ruled with full sovereignty a nation that was already constituted with it. Congress did not challenge Lincoln's war power, even though he used it against American states, and it was the main power he had as head of a government that was not set up to be fully sovereign. It was difficult for Lincoln to act with the authority of a leader of a sovereign state because his revolutionary goal was to make a government sovereign that was not sovereign. It is debatable whether he ever reached the level of power of a Napoleon or a Cromwell but it is certain that he steadily gained power even after the early defeats of his armies and as his armies bludgeoned their way to the final victory, he became very nearly a fully endowed tyrant.

After the defeat of the Federal army's first invasion of Virginia at Manassas, Lincoln selected George McClellan, a highly experienced soldier, to be general of the massive army he was assembling in Washington to crush Virginia and capture Richmond, the capital of Virginia and also the new capital of the Confederacy of 11 seceded states. Lincoln's appointment of McClellan was strange both because he was commanding him to invade American states in the south with troops from American states in the north and because both men sensed that the power the president handed over to his general was unheard of with no precedent, certainly unconstitutional, and possibly treasonable. The thousands and thousands of young men assembling in Washington and training for war increased the tension that grew up between Lincoln and McClellan because the general of the northern forces felt *he* had become sovereign as head of the army and because he knew from his experiences in wars that the odd new sovereign authority placed on his shoulders must lead to the deaths of thousands of young men without any previous experience of war on the fields of Virginia. McClellan, a well educated man who had been an observer in 1855 at the Crimean War, treated the president who had little formal education with a kind of free and easy indifference that was certainly disrespectful and sometimes changed to contempt. McClellan hesitated to go to war stalling month after month frustrating Lincoln by delay after delay. For 8 months while McClellan hesitated to move his army into Virginia, Lincoln was assailed politely but firmly by radical republicans frustrated that he would not set the army in motion and command it to march south and capture Richmond. McClellan moved, when he finally moved on March 17, 1862, not straight ahead south where there were easily defensible rivers in his path but instead by ships down the Potomac River to a safe and easy landing of his troops on the peninsula south of Richmond. McClellan hoped and hoped that this massive display of force would somehow bring the leaders of both unions of states to their senses and compel some sudden compromise and armistice that would make armed conflict unnecessary. No general ever lead an army to war with less interest in fighting and his refusal to commit his forces fully in battle after battle against points in the defensive lines of his opponents that might have led to victory prove to anyone capable of real objectivity that McClellan both in the Peninsula Campaign in Virginia and at the next battle he fought at Antietam in Maryland did not want war because it was a useless destruction of young men's lives and because it was a war between Americans that was unjustified and totally at odds with all their previous history together in a brotherly and perpetual union of states.

General Lee drove General McClellan's army out of Virginia after Lincoln's second invasion but strangely it made Lincoln's authority stronger. McClellan was cautious in the deployment of his forces always trying to avoid the bludgeoning type of warfare that Lincoln later in the war got General Grant to wage, but he had conducted successfully a large orderly campaign on enemy territory and his troops, even though inexperienced, had fought well. When he met face to face with Lincoln who had traveled by ship down to the peninsula in Virginia to confer with him, he was no longer contemptuous and now showed respect for Lincoln. He realized that the president whom he had previously treated as a weak and unknowing federal official had somehow put together for action a vast new assemblage of men united in state regiments and divisions in a war that now must continue to some fatal conclusion. On both sides of the battle lines, Lincoln, the enemy of state sovereignty, had created out of nowhere a deadly means for every state in the union to act because of the war for a few short years as a nation-state. McClellan's men loved him because he had used his military knowledge to keep them in good order and to avoid sometimes the useless and unnecessary shedding of blood. They loved him his men and they were from many different states and proud with something like real nationalistic sentiment to represent their state and win glory for their state. Lincoln somehow had set North Carolinians against Rhode Islanders, New Yorkers against Texans, Georgians against New Hampshire men. Men from 34 sovereign states were out on battlefields fighting state against state and yet the man who had started the deadly interstate hubbub was not located in any state and was not the head of the government of any state. Before Lincoln's war men found an indirect outlet for the nationalistic feelings that were denied them as members of states with limited sovereignty by expressing publicly passionate sentiments for and against slavery but such protests failed to satisfy their need for some real direct outlet to ease what troubled their spirits. Men north and south felt that the union had developed so successfully and added so many states that it was out of balance. War could possibly create a new lack of balance but some wanted it anyway and Lincoln provided the war even though it had no real reason to exist. The New England writer Nathanial Hawthorne had a sharp eye and always spoke the truth. "I don't understand what the war is about," he said. "The southerners are not my fellow countrymen. We should just give them a good thrashing and kick them out of the union." No one knew what the war was about better than Lincoln. He had a plan for a new nation and he needed a war to gain sovereignty for the federal government to execute his plan. General McClellan in his Peninsula Campaign had acted as the main actor in the mighty strange new drama that had unfolded itself before his eyes. He understood at last that a radical new future was on the way for the United States and that an American had to either become an actor in the drama and applaud heartily for its author and the nation he was creating or keep off the stage with no connection to the radical new historical forces pushing the union to a new form and a new future. Shortly after Lincoln ended his visit to him on the peninsula in Virginia, General McClellan wrote a letter to him expressing the extent of his changed sentiments towards his leader. Before he had been critical and disdainful of Lincoln, but now he addressed him as his sovereign, like a Roman general voicing his loyal support for his emperor. He wrote in part of his letter, "Let neither military disaster, political faction or foreign war shake your settled purpose to enforce the equal operation of the laws of the United States upon the people of every state. The time has come when the Government must determine upon a civil and military policy, covering the whole ground of our national trouble. The responsibility of determining, declaring and supporting such civil and military policy and of directing the whole course of national affairs in regard to the rebellion, must now be assumed and exercised by you or our cause will be lost. The Constitution gives you power sufficient even for the present terrible exigency." McClellan perceived clearly what Lincoln had accomplished. He had forced South Carolina to bombard Fort Sumter. He had forced by his proclamation of April 15 Virginia and three more slave states to secede. The eleven seceded states by defending themselves against northern armies had made Lincoln the sovereign leader of a sovereign Federal Government.

General McClellan wrote his letter in the very midst of his battle against men defending Virginia. Virginia's defense of itself was tragic not only because it could not win the war even with the extraordinary courage and zeal of its defenders but also because some of her defenders were slave owners and all of them were condemned by history to defend at the same time both state sovereignty and slavery. Any student who now at the beginning of the twenty-first century wishes to probe and discover the issues of the Civil War should begin his/her inquiry by simply reading the stories of the battles in Virginia. The southerners fought so fiercely and bravely that their victories against superior numbers should make any modern student start wondering why men came from 10 of the 11 seceded states to help defend Virginia and why in the world and for what reason anyway they were fighting. But the modern student can not reach the heart of the matter because his/her eyes are blurred knowing from the start of the inquiry that the men fighting in defense of Virginia were indeed fighting to continue human slavery. General Thomas Jackson, a Virginian that southerners called "Stonewall" Jackson, was the most celebrated hero of the conflict. Englishmen admired him so greatly that they collected money and set up a statue of Jackson that a student can see today on the grounds in Richmond near the Virginia statehouse. But the student can also today visit the Stonewall Jackson House, a museum in Lexington Virginia located in the house Jackson lived in with his wife when he was a professor before the war at the Virginia Military Institute in Lexington. Every day Thomas Jackson returned home from his teaching and read his bible. He was such a devout Protestant that one day during his successful campaign in the Shenandoah Valley against federal forces, he hesitated to fight at an opportune moment because it was the Sabbath. Jackson read and studied his bible every day but he also gave orders every day to his ten slaves. Every day he took command of the lives of ten human beings and used them as property with a status barely above animals. It is easy to convince a student outraged by southern slavery that Lincoln's war was a war to end slavery because the end of slavery was the indirect result. Lincoln promoted himself as an up and coming politician by appearing to be morally against slavery and he secured the Republican nomination for president by making himself a champion in his speeches against allowing slavery in the new western territories while at the same time making it clear that he was not against slavery in states where it already existed. He held the state of Maryland under martial law throughout the war and could have used his dictatorial power to proclaim slavery unlawful in a state under his control. But Lincoln did not move against slavery in places where he had power over it. Instead he cleverly issued an Emancipation Proclamation in 1863 that freed slaves in southern states who belonged to masters who had taken up arms to defend themselves from his federal armies. He had no power under the Constitution to free slaves and his Emancipation Proclamation freed slaves only in places where his war power that he was using tyrannically had no power.

General Lee took his army north into Pennsylvania to Gettysburg. He gambled that he could perhaps win a decisive victory in a northern state and end the war because he knew he could not gather sufficient men and resources in Virginia to keep defeating and pushing back large well supplied invading armies. The array of soldiers lined up for battle under the bright July sun on the open green fields of Gettysburg was splendid. In the morning before the cannons and rifles exploded forth their deadly missiles, men from all over the union, from every state in the union, stood looking across the open space between them at peace. Abraham Lincoln had assembled them there. He assembled men from every state in the union and on that morning for a few moments before the killing began they were truly the nation, they were truly in America because the nation exists and America exists wherever Americans are alive together free men among free men enjoying peace with their freedom guaranteed by a just perpetual union. Then the cannons exploded and the rifles fired and the union was dead and the nation was dead and peace was dead along with the Americans who were soon lying on the ground dead. If only Lincoln had found some common enemy for them to fight, they might have stood united as a nation that morning, like the ancient Greeks united as a nation by their war against Troy, united as Americans fighting an enemy. But Lincoln could find no enemy for Americans to fight against except one another.

4

A union of 34 sovereign states can not logically be understood as a nation. But Washington had assumed enough sovereign power to defeat in war eleven of the states and no power existed in the restored union to oppose further power-grabbing. It seemed best to understand that the radical power shift in the union had resulted in a nation. Historians helped unify the altered union by rewriting American history with the central idea that there had somehow always been a nation even back in the seventeenth century. School children soon began pledging allegiance every school day to the nation. The Pledge of Allegiance expressed the new radical state of the union thus: "I pledge allegiance to the flag of the United States of America and to the republic for which it stands, one nation indivisible with liberty and justice for all." The thirteen red and white stripes stretched across the flag represent the 13 original states of the union. The stars on the flag represent the 13 original states and all subsequent states admitted to the union by bills passed by the Congress. The stars and stripes express the union's complexity. The Pledge of Allegiance simplifies it. It states that all the states taken together are a republic. And it states that this republic is one nation.

The federal army held the 11 defeated confederate states under martial law for five years. The military power that the Federal Government possessed was something that every American now reckoned with and feared. Everyone knew that Washington could use its army against whomever it wished and that it was further solidifying its power with a federal police force and federal prisons. The radical republicans in power in Congress after Lincoln's assassination had supported the war and now did everything possible to further reduce state sovereignty. First they tried to impeach Andrew Johnson, Lincoln's vice-president, who succeeded him to the presidency. He was a southerner who had been against the south taking up arms. He wanted the complex new governmental apparatus created by the war to go back to as it had been before the war. He wanted to put the genie that Lincoln had let out of the bottle back in the bottle. President Johnson had defied a piece of unconstitutional legislation passed by the radical republicans and survived the trial by impeachment in Congress that resulted by one vote. Lincoln had used the slavery issue to gain the presidency and to start a war to cripple state sovereignty. The Republicans after the war continued to use slavery as a weapon against state sovereignty. With the 11 defeated states who had seceded conquered and living under martial law without representation in Congress, the 13th amendment abolishing slavery was passed by Congress in 1865 and ratified by the states who had remained faithful to the union. It was a welcome and joyous act but it was also the first amendment to the Constitution that was *against* state sovereignty. The 12th amendment had merely adjusted the electoral college's procedure but amendments 1 to 11 had either *increased* state sovereignty or protected individual rights. In the moral joy that hopefully was universal, few noticed that the 13th amendment also radically reordered the economies of 15 former slave states and opened up for the savage new dog-eat-dog free-wheeling economy 15 states with severely reduced sovereignty for pristine new business adventures. In addition, the slaves granted freedom were not granted expressly in the language of the 13th amendment first-class citizenship which was their due and was vitally necessary. White men were again exploiting black men for their profit at least indirectly.

The 14th amendment in 1865 does expressly guarantee former slaves and any person born in the United States citizenship in both the United States and the state where they reside. This is established in the very first sentence in Section 1., "All persons born or naturalized in the United States, and subject to the jurisdiction thereof, are citizens of the United States and of the State wherein they reside." The new radical approach of the Republicans begins in this line which asserts falsely that a person can be born in the United States when in reality a person can be born only in a state. It then asserts that all persons so born are subject to the jurisdiction of the United States. This truth borders on falsity because while we are indeed subject to the jurisdiction of the United States we are subject to such power only in laws created to execute the powers of Congress spelled out specifically in the Constitution and not in unspecified areas. The sentence avoids mentioning the limited jurisdiction of Congress because it was now the business of Republicans to extend it. The 14th amendment establishes for its message the existence of 5 entities, "persons", "the United States", "the jurisdiction thereof", "citizens" and "the State wherein they reside". We are no longer hearing the language of the Constitution which speaks of "The government of the United States." The language now speaks of the United States as an entity separate from the states and of "the jurisdiction thereof". "Jurisdiction" is synonymous with "power" and here it comes as close as possible to meaning "sovereignty" without violating the letter of the Constitution. This opening sentence is simply the first attack in the 14th amendment on the sovereignty of the states, a political power radically weakened by the Civil War and now transferred to the Federal Government. The other radical step in the sentence is the assertion that we now have double citizenship, state citizenship and federal citizenship. The Constitution uses the word "citizens" twice and both times referring to state citizenship. Our new federal citizenship grants us privileges and immunities against the power of a state to make or enforce its laws. This is indeed a new world, this is Lincoln's new nation. Federal cannons are again firing at men standing up for their right to live in sovereign states. The very next sentence of Article 1. protects the former slaves, now citizens, and all persons subject to the jurisdiction of Washington, from the unjust use of sovereignty in the state where they may reside by attacking state sovereignty directly: "No State shall make or enforce any law which shall abridge the privileges or immunities of citizens of the

United States; nor shall any State deprive any person of life, liberty, or property, without due process of law; nor deny to any person within its jurisdiction the equal protection of the laws." We still live in sovereign states but their citizens are protected from state authority by radically increased individual rights designed to reduce state power.

However the passing of the 14th amendment reveals one of the avenues politicians planned to use to accede to national sovereign power, the legal system. Before the Civil War, both Federal and State laws were used to enforce policies. The legal system did most of the practical business of deciding rights and enforcing them by court decisions. The Federal circuit courts made regular appearances at various locations in all the states and judged state and federal laws on appeal. The Republicans planned to use the system just as it existed in its present form to either allow state laws that favored their policies or else strike down unfavorable laws using the power of federal courts to strike down decisions of lower state courts. The top of the system was the Supreme Court in Washington. It possessed one third of federal power because it could strike down any law State or Federal passed at any level of government. The power of the Supreme Court was based solely on its right to interpret the Constitution. This meant that the Republicans or politicians of any party were forced at the risk of rendering null and void the entire legal system to obey the Constitution.

Postwar Republicans saw clearly that to rule the United States from the top down they had to amend the Constitution in a radical manner and also influence judges appointed to the federal courts and especially to the Supreme Court to interpret the Constitution broadly enough to strike down state laws that empowered policies that went against federal power. Money-grubbing and the other uncouth practices of bureaucrats, lobbyists and office holders in Washington were directly supported by hundreds of federal court decisions based on the 14th amendment and irreverent interpretations of the Constitution. Abusive use of the court system directly supported rich bankers and industrialists by striking down state laws that supported unionization of workers or tried to regulate even moderately the unbridled savage survival-of-the-fittest industrialized capitalism of the postwar period. Rich men controlled all the branches of all the governments both state and federal and used every political trick to keep power out of the hands of the average American and immigrants laboring in the dog-eat-dog industrial hell of the late nineteenth century. The "equal protection of the laws" guaranteed to citizens by the 14th amendment did not protect striking workers from the clubs of policemen.

Politically there was no hope for the average American because Washington controlled enough central power either with its own laws or with state laws to crush political dissent. Individually however there was plenty of hope. The new religion that thrived in the late-nineteenth-century industrial jungles preached that poverty was shameful and evil and riches blessed. People struggled to improve their lot by making money. They ascended if they could the stairs to the divine temples where the rich lived in bliss. On their way up, like the rich, they did not look down and back at the millions of Americans that the industrial hell had defeated and held prisoners in the hell fire of poverty.

The Federal Government had increased national power but it did little to give the nation that Lincoln had spoken of in the Gettysburg Address a definite shape. The Constitution was amended and reinterpreted but it was still in force with individual rights of citizens written down and valid enough to protect citizens' rights in courts. The Constitution still restricted the actions of federal politicians and they were very willing to accept the restrictions since it often meant they were free to do little or nothing nationally and everything they could for themselves. Federal power remained divided among the three branches of government, the executive, the legislative and the judicial. This prevented the easy exercise of power and created conflict and hatred among the branches. Cabinet officers hated the indecency and egotism of Senators who used their powers extravagantly in their own interest. It was clear to cabinet officers that senatorial power had to be reduced if the government was to work for some national benefit and not just for the crass benefits senators sought for themselves and their cronies. But in the give and take of the fight for power, national benefits were the last benefits politicians thought about and they thought about them rarely or not at all. As for members of the House of Representatives, a cabinet officer told Henry Adams, a New Englander who wrote his observations about postwar Washington, "You can't use tact with a Congressman! A Congressman is a hog! You must take a stick and hit him on the snout!" Washington was not taking shape in some new form that would directly benefit the nation but most Americans had little to do with Washington anyway and they went about the business of creating their nation on their own.

A good part of the new nation was composed of English-speaking Anglo-Saxon Protestants. The first truth that took solid root in this group's mind and soul after the Civil War was that they should go about their business as fully as possible individually and that they should never wish or hope that anything would ever be done for their individual benefit by the government in Washington ever. They wanted as little as possible to do with Washington and they considered it an expression of a grave moral weakness, almost of a sinful condition, if anyone expected anything from it. Protestants in the south lived for 5 years under martial law imposed on them by Washington's armies. Protestants in the north had sent their sons to their death in Washington's armies and gained for themselves the same reduced sovereignty in their states that the radical republics were imposing. They knew that nothing could come from Washington except more power for Washington and less for themselves. They knew that the only power they had was the power they found in themselves. That was where the new nation was taking root. That was where the nation existed. In the souls of Anglo-Saxon Protestants.

Nation-states in Europe thrived partly because beyond their national borders lived alien peoples speaking languages incomprehensible to their native people. The native people in America after the Civil War were soon surrounded by vast numbers of former natives of European nation-states speaking incomprehensible languages. Over 20 million European immigrants came to America between 1870 and 1910. Native Americans who were Anglo-Saxon and Protestant were already deeply united culturally and religiously and they did not need European immigrants speaking many incomprehensible languages to unite them. But foreigners living and working among them did help to unite them more solidly. American Protestants had no nation-state but they were millions strong with individualistic values that united them and gave their lives purpose as more and more Europeans crossed United States borders to work in one of the states whose numbers kept increasing with the continual admission of new states.

The national business of the Federal Government in the revolutionary industrial development of America from the Civil War to 1900 became the business not of creating national policies directing the development but of interfering in the development wherever and whenever it chose in the interest of whomever it chose. It decided to be not a national leader but a national referee. Instead of using its new authority to pass federal laws benefiting all the citizens of the nation, it used the Supreme Court to nullify state laws. It's business was not to govern but to interfere with governments. Generally speaking, it interfered in this way mainly to aid the clever organizers and administrators of the new corporations busy exploiting the new machines that could vastly increase industrial production and extend the distribution of new products across the continent using the new intercontinental railroads. Captains of the new industries bribed state and national politicians to get laws they wanted. The Central Pacific railroad spent only $200,000 in Washington on bribes and received 9 million acres of free land plus bonds worth millions. The new monopolies of industrial, railroad and oil companies did arouse the anger of Americans and they were disturbed that Washington had its hands in on the action and was not by any means an objective and indifferent referee. Protests of all kinds rose up against the gigantic trusts and new monopolies and some politicians represented themselves as trust busters to earn election to an office in Washington and then to do nothing. In fact, there was little to do. Washington understood that it required too much effort and an expensive use of its power to unify a nation composed of so many states. The big corporations were unifying the nation and Washington sat back and merely refereed what they were doing. America was not getting a national government of the kind that set and enforced national policies. Because Washington interfered so often to aid this or that petty and selfish interest, few noticed that Washington had given itself the power to interfere in the doings of the nation rather than to be itself the tyrannical ruler of the nation. And since it had great power and it could use it as it pleased, it also escaped the notice of most citizens that this meant that it might or it could interfere in the doings of the nation *to produce good.*

Native Protestant Americans did not want anything from Washington, even good, and the millions of immigrants understood nothing about American history and politics. It is possible that some Anglo-Saxon Americans in their soul of souls never accepted even that they lived in a nation and every immigrant knew the slogan that passed among them universally and was equivalent to not living in a nation, "America is a free country". As America rolled on through the most extraordinary industrial revolution ever witnessed on the planet, Washington became more and more aloof from the action. Only an elite few had access to federal power and the majority excluded from federal power tried to remain as indifferent to it as possible. America was a free country for immigrants and native Anglo-Saxon Protestants did not want any part of Washington, so what was Washington to do but be what both groups wanted, a referee? At home, Washington was losing the role Abraham Lincoln had bequeathed to it as the champion of a new nation even though it had increased national power and kept increasing it. At least abroad its status as a national government was clear and direct because Washington's diplomats had relations with the heads of state of all the nation-states and empires in the world who accepted the United States worldwide as a nation and assumed that it was one at home too.

Washington had the power granted in the Constitution to regulate commerce among the states. This meant that no state could close its borders to interstate commerce. The Supreme Court used the 14th amendment 288 times between 1870 and 1910 in judgments in favor of corporations to assure their freedom to do business in states without excessive state regulation. Industry roared ahead savage and uncontrolled by any government. Interlocking networks of corporations developed to a degree that was simply astounding putting control of the corporate part of the American economy in the hands of a small number of men. In Europe, every nation-state limited the expansion of its industrial corporations by national borders. The major industries like steel production were duplicated in many nation-states and protected by international tariffs. In America, 14 new states were admitted to the union between 1864 and 1910. In Europe, the middle-class industrialists shut themselves up behind borders within states and created laws that enriched themselves and impoverished workers. In America, the middle-class industrialists freely seized mineral wealth in any state where it existed and expanded industrial production across a continent just as if there were no state borders anywhere. Workers' rights were repressed by governments in America as well as in Europe but American workers with the same small portion of the pie as in Europe earned more money because the pie was bigger and growing rapidly because capitalistic greed was not imprisoned behind nation-state borders. People worldwide read about the bounteous economic expansion in America with awe. Of those who noted the expansion in America of the states to 48, few reacted to it with appropriate awe. All the 48 states still had democratic governments and their governments created for their citizens the same civilized public necessities that other states in the world created for their citizens. The difference was that foreign states worldwide were fully sovereign and rarely democratic. 48 American states knew that they would never be as sovereign as they were before the Civil War but they were learning under the domination of Washington that their limited sovereignty did not mean that they could not enjoy democratic state governments.

America after the Civil War was developing politically in shapes that had never before appeared anywhere and that were difficult to understand because they were so revolutionary. Everyone now accepted that Washington was the head of a nation but this acceptance was partly in some the hope that Washington could somehow gain control of the new shapes and fit them into meaningful forms that could be universally understood. Washington had gained greater sovereignty but it was not enough to manage the revolution. The states had lost sovereignty but they controlled the shape of things within their borders in a settled fashion. Washington learned as the century whirled out of control towards its end that it was best for its security that it act aloofly and universally. It was a solid player already in the universal interplay among nations worldwide.

It decided to act universally at home too. For most of the latter part of the nineteenth century, it struck the pose of an imperial government. It flew off into the higher realms of politics where rulers spoke benignly in a universal style that provided them the pretense of not ruling even though they had the power to jump into the action whenever they wished and to rule what they chose to rule. The flight of Washington to an aloof status was paralleled in American culture by the creation of two new religions. Christian Science was a latter-day development of New England Transcendentalism which had had its roots firmly in the material world. Christian Science believed that only spirit was real and the material world was an illusion. The new Mormon religion taught that rather than believe in Christ and miraculously discover the world of God, believers should instead raise the quality of their behavior to become the equal of Christ. In both cases the self was lifted to a level of spirituality that was but a vain attempt to escape the real human condition.

5

In 1889, William Torrey Harris was appointed US Commissioner of Education. Harris was a devotee of Hegelian philosophy and he used his knowledge of the philosopher Hegel's dialectic to understand the logical pattern behind changes that appeared to be illogical. A positive action, a thesis, always produced some negative reaction, an antithesis, that produced in turn a new negation that took on a positive form, a synthesis. The dialectic made a series of actions that seemed in themselves devoid of meaning meaningful. Harris, a high official of the Federal Government, would have found it simple to apply the Hegelian dialectic to understand what had lead to the Civil War. The thesis was the opening up of new territories for statehood to the west of the Mississippi River. The antithesis was the refusal on the part of radical Republicans in the north to allow slavery in the new territories and the election of Lincoln as president who championed their position. The synthesis was the Civil War and the new America that resulted. Harris perceived the deep alienation in Americans in the years after the war caused by their sense of being alone and isolated without any fixed identity on a huge continent cut off from the center of power in Washington. Their alienation might become a danger to the upper-class Anglo-Saxon society in which men like Harris lived richly and securely. "The highest ideal of a civilization," he wrote, "is that of a civilization that is engaged constantly in elevating lower classes of people into participation of all that is good and reasonable and perpetually increasing at the same time their self-activity. Such a civilization we have a right to enforce on this earth". His means of enforcing it was public education. To the general alienation visible everywhere in the new every-man-for-himself postwar America, he proposed no less than self-alienation in schools. "Ninety-nine [students] out of a hundred," he wrote, " are automata, careful to walk in prescribed paths, careful to follow the prescribed custom. This is not an accident but the result of substantial education, which, scientifically defined, is the subsumption of the individual." Alienation already existed to an extreme degree in the new America. He proposed, as US Commissioner of Education, that self-alienation should be the main business of the classroom. "The great purpose of school can be realized better in dark, airless, ugly places ... It is to master the physical self, to transcend the beauty of nature. School should develop the power to withdraw from the external world."

The upper classes withdrew from the harsh new external world of postwar unregimented free-wheeling capitalism to ships sailing to Europe where their immersion in various forms of higher culture allowed them to self-alienate themselves comfortably and enjoyably. The Americans left behind because of their meager means were condemned to self-alienate themselves at home and learn the forms of obedience necessary to produce an orderly society by submitting to the regimented way of life taught in public schools.

Self-alienation in Hegelian philosophy is a necessary moment in the development of spirit. The middle-class rationalistic philosophy of the eighteenth century was well established in Hegel's time (1770-1831) and he tried to carry it forward to a new stage of development. For him there was no such thing as static spirit. The earlier middle-class philoso-phers had liked to fit spirit into nicely rationalized fixed forms that were permanent and eternal. For Hegel, rationality and spirit are the same thing and they are constantly developing through negations and affir-mations and negations. William Harris understood as did many other Anglo-Saxon thinkers that middle-class values alone existed or deserved to exist in America and in order to enforce them on the lower-class masses of native Americans and on the lower-class sons and daughters of new immigrants, development of their spirit was necessary through self-alienation in schools and regimented orientations to higher forms of middle-class cultural experiences made available in popular mass educational movements like the Chautauqua movement. Begun in 1874, Chautauqua developed from the practice of camp meetings in the summer to give crowds of people religious instruction. It added secular instruction giving courses in the arts, sciences and the humanities. The movement flourished propelling Americans hungry for culture to higher levels of self-alienation and to discoveries of middle-class values that were essential for advancement and success in the new America. Droves of people desired passionately to transcend the ordinary dog-eat-dog life offered them by working regimented in the work-a-day hell caused by survival-of-the-fittest industrialized American capitalism. If you did not transcend your life by some form of self-alienation, you had to live with the kind of self that once thrived naturally in the freedom and wilderness of a previous America and was now doomed to defeat and impotence.

These middle-class values were not new. In fact, they had been developing in Europe since the eleventh century. In a society of nobles on the one hand and serfs on the other, men began escaping hundreds of years ago to towns which began establishing themselves all over Europe. Men living and working in the towns, burgs, became members of a new class midway between the nobles and the serfs, they were the bourgeois, the new *middle* class. They were entrepreneurs, craftsmen, manufacturers, artists who employed workers. They established rights for themselves separate from the rights of nobles and serfs. At first, the merchants and producers in the towns worked in harmony with their workers. Both groups had solidly established rights and were members of guilds. The prices of goods produced were strictly fixed. Wages were fixed. The church went so far as to declare profits sinful. Workers had many days off at public holidays and holy days. Even the destitute poor had rights to public lands where they could keep a cow and had the right to gather gleanings left over after harvests to feed themselves and to build themselves thatched huts. But the bourgeoisie over a long period set themselves up as a separate class because it was only by alienating themselves from fellow members of their communities that they could become rich. The main road to riches was cheating. Prices of manufactured goods were fixed and products were of equal intrinsic value so one merchant became wealthier than others in his guild by secretly lowering the quality of his product. This produced excess money in the hands of individuals, capital that they could reinvest and make more money. Townsmen with money built themselves rich homes and displayed themselves in fine new clothes that set them apart from the clothes of nobles, peasants and workers. The individual entrepreneur rose to prominence. The political power they gained as town leaders gradually allowed them to eliminate the customs with the force of law that had protected workers and peasants. The bourgeoisie made still more money by getting rid of public holidays and by gaining the right to work workers longer hours and by paying them less. In England, Anglo-Saxon law based partly on custom continued but in France bourgeois lawyers studied Roman law which had no roots in custom and was based solely on authority. Lawyers changed laws to protect the newly rich bourgeois entrepreneurs who got even richer by the protection afforded them by the laws they instituted. Culturally, the great epiphanies of middle-class culture were Protestantism and the Renaissance. Merchants in towns always searching for new technologies learned to print and spread around religious writings so that the new individualistic middle class could start examining its religious beliefs individually. Middle-class lawyers needed to know Latin to understand Roman law and apply it to revolutionary effect in their nation-states. Culturally, this need helped inspire the creative outbursts of the Renaissance based on a rediscovery of the literature and art of the ancient world. Latin was essential to the educated bourgeois because it enabled him to Latinize his native language so that he could speak with a vocabulary and a new style that was incomprehensible to the masses. Alienation from the masses in every possible way was the goal of the bourgeoisie. The new rich were unique with an unique new basis of wealth and their goal was to remain unique in blissful self-alienation. The English were the first Europeans to create a nation-state with a government that integrated the nobility and the bourgeoisie with laws devoted to protecting the old rich and the newly rich. Their nation-state became powerful because its government protected by law the wealth and alienation of the rich and enabled England to be the scene of the first industrial revolution in the seventeenth century. In Europe the English success in creating a powerful nation-state caused a rush all over the continent to establish modern nation-states everywhere as soon as possible.

The government of the European nation-state was run by the middle class for the middle class. No attempt was ever made to make the masses of people middle class although middle-class elite schools and universities with knowledge oriented to middle-class values and towards the middle-class scientific and rational slant of knowledge did allow a scattering of men from the masses to become bourgeois. But in Europe the middle-class governments were against the masses to such en extent that in the early part of the nineteenth century a man working in France from dawn to dusk six days a week in a factory could not earn enough to feed himself and his family. The central governments in Europe were against the masses and they called up against themselves revolution after revolution which they put down brutally. In the United States, Lincoln's revolution gave men with middle-class values solid control of the central government but the difference was that the new political rulers and their educated and rich adherents and beneficiaries understood that they could grow stronger and prosper richly in the new America by forcing all the members of the lower classes to live only with middle-class values. They could embody middle- class values in all their people, values which were revolutionary in origin and when spread universally to everyone over a large continent with 45 states must make a great positive revolution. In European nation-states, a small minority controlled the central government always in danger of revolution from within and attacks from enemy nation-states from without. In America, no nation-state existed and the central government was controlled mainly by rich educated middle-class Anglo-Saxons. It was isolated from any possible revolution or attack because it was surrounded by 45 states with severely reduced sovereignty and with populations with no choice but to adopt their rulers' values because in a society without nobles or peasants no other values had any value.

By Harris's time in 1889, something like a new nation was taking a more definite shape. The Federal Government was now *the* government and just as pupils in American schools had to be regimented to learn new cultural values, the states also had to submit to regimentation, regimentation by Washington, and learn new political values. It is hard for a student to enter a public school with a child's vivid imagination and leave it after 12 years of regimentation with middle-class values forced into his brain. But he does leave with values, solid reasonable workable values. He also has large doses of universal values meshed in with pedestrian notions of how to discipline himself to take advantage of circumstances around him in the external world for his profit. It is hard for our states to be regimented too after their beginnings when they set off explosions to celebrate on the fourth of July 1776 their independence and after they enjoyed for almost a hundred years a political condition close to full sovereignty. In the late nineteenth century, Americans were forced to take upon themselves a new identity and although no vital sense of a national identity came to them from Washington at the top of the ladder, they did discover an identity that gave them power and purpose in the new America. They discovered that it was useless to act guided by any sort of universal or national standards of behavior but that on the individual level middle-class values worked. Individuals discovered individually what Americans call "the work ethic" and although it was an individual phenomenon it was so universal that, reinforced by middle-class indoctrination in the public schools, it helped unite the new nation. Rich industrialists and bankers cared nothing about any national or state government's power unless it freed them to make huge profits. They used politicians and the courts to help them ruthlessly gain monopolistic control of markets and keep wages as low as possible. It was every man and every business for themselves in the survival-of-the-fittest economic jungles. In the economic arena no one was united with anyone and this lack of unity made middle-class values the only solid weapon against defeat and produced an overall unity that was revolutionary but at the same time perfectly adapted to a union of states with a government at the top that was not much more than a ref-eree. "America" and "the nation" were words that were used abstractly and carelessly to suit any purpose but they were now finding contexts that gave them sometimes positive meaning. There was no "America" anywhere but it did seem more and more like a real place. There was no "nation" that existed like nation-states in some exact political, ethnic and territorial context but still Washington was a central government and it was solidly in control of the states. It began to be meaningful to call Washington the government of the nation because the unity it somehow produced among 45 states with capitalistic entrepreneurs running wild everywhere was amazing. By 1900, 45 states with separate independent democratic governments stretched across a great continent from the Atlantic to the Pacific Ocean with open borders and with state citizenship open to any American in any of the states merely by taking up residence in one of them. This wonderful extraordinary political phenomenon, unknown anywhere else in the world, had to have some simple and easy name to describe it even though its complexity and its extraordinary on-going revolutionary development was indescribable in simple terms. Native Americans and immigrants and everyone outside the United States called it America. It was not one fixed place but nonetheless seemed to be a place. It was made up of many peoples but there seemed nonetheless to be one people. It had many democratic governments in many states but it had one government in Washington that was *the* government. There was enough unity to say that America was one nation.

6

But the American Constitution still told the new nation in America what political powers its central government and its states possessed. The Republicans feared the power of the Constitution and had rushed to amend it for their radical aims but they were forced to accept as law what they could not amend. The degree of sovereignty that the Federal Government now possessed was the result of the military power it displayed in the Civil War added to the limited sovereign powers granted it in the Constitution. It expanded its powers by limiting state power by the 13th and 14th amendments and by using the court system to strike down state laws that opposed federal policies or tried to regulate business practices. It also increased its power by regimenting students in public schools and by influencing citizens to accept versions of American history slanted radically towards the idea that America was a nation like any other nation with a national government in a capital city, Washington D.C.. Everything worked against the states including the political propaganda doled out in the public schools which rarely mentioned the effect on American life of the political powers of state governments. Everything worked against the sovereignty of the states and towards the sovereignty of the Federal Government. Everything except the Constitution. The Constitution does not assign full sovereign power to any state. Instead it takes sovereign powers away from all the states of the union and gives sovereign powers to a central government that is not located in a state. It not only refuses to the Federal Government the status of a state but also separates its power among three branches, the executive, the legislative and the judicial. The genius of the Constitution is that its design makes no government completely sovereign and forces every one of them to be democratic. The Federal Government marched ahead after the Civil War towards the status of a national state without being a state and the states, weakened by the war, believed they had lost the status as states with nearly full sovereign power that they had had before the war. The rush towards the creation of America as a nation was based on the fiction that the Constitution had created a national government located in Washington D.C.. At the same time, the states suffered from the fiction that the ratification of the Constitution had left them with nearly full sovereign power when in reality such a degree of power had already been taken away from them by the Constitution. The Constitution had limited the powers of all American governments to such a radical degree that they were all doomed forever to be capable of functioning only as democracies.

In the public schools we were never infused by our teachers with the deeper patriotic feelings that might have been aroused in us if we had learned that the true majesty and glory of the new nation derived from the successful union of 48 states with open borders and democratic governments. We were educated as though it were a matter of indifference if we happened to live in Massachusetts or Louisiana. We all knew we lived in one state and not another and that there were 48 states but it meant nothing to us. We did not *feel* a connection with any state. We were not confused however because we were very secure being Americans and living in America. America was everywhere and nowhere but still it existed and there were people off in the blue somewhere running its government so everything was fine.

The idea of not being loyal to the American government in Washington and to America and everything we learned about America in our history books never entered our minds. The government in Washington had never built and funded a public school or university in any state but we had schools and universities and we didn't care where they came from. Washington had never built and funded a public hospital in a state but we had hospitals. It had never built and sustained state roads or state transportation systems but we had them. It had never established and maintained libraries outside of the District of Columbia but we had libraries in every town and city. It had never established and funded police and fire services outside the District of Columbia but we had them. Washington had no power to register births and deaths because a United States citizen can be born and die only in one state of many states but that was something that went on everywhere anyway and was not a problem. Our national government had no power to marry couples under civil law but marriages took place all the time and what government legalized them was not a problem at all. Banks and corporations were incorporated exclusively in states by state law and states alone certified and oversaw hundreds of professions and public organizations and public activities but these again were activities for us that just somehow went on. We did not care either that the state we happened to live in had power to do just about everything necessary for the public good as in any other state anywhere in the world and it did not bother us that it had no power to wage war or conduct diplomatic activities with other states. We were Americans. We were living in America. That was what counted. That was the only thing that counted.

No one who wrote our history books dared to look realistically and intelligently at American history and tell us what had really happened. A simple look at the map of the United States with just a basic general knowledge of key events in our past should have told us that an extraordinary revolutionary unfolding and development of humanity unlike anything in its past had somehow happened on our continent. A look at a map of the thirteen original states stretched north and south along the Atlantic Ocean should have taught us that our rebellion and freedom from England with its super powerful navy and army would have been impossible unless England had simply decided finally to let us go and be rid of us. England had wars all over the globe to fight in the eighteenth century and she was tired of trying to conquer and rule crude uneducated swarms of white men with their black slaves scattered about in a vast wilderness. England understood that humanity's adventure in America would never work and she let us go free to learn for ourselves that we were condemned in advance to futility. Historians told us that George Washington and Americans won the war against England and they did not mention when possible that 4000 experienced French soldiers and the French fleet produced the victory at Yorktown. Instead of identifying the settlers in America and their hundreds of racial backgrounds, our historians focused on the devout life-style of Anglo-Saxon religious pilgrims in the northeast who planted on our shores the notion that religion and the search for material enjoyments and economic profits can work together harmoniously. We treated native Americans very badly, cruelly, and we owned black and white slaves north and south but historians quickly passed over our Indian Wars which were genocidal and they did not emphasize that the descendants of the pilgrims made piles of money with their ships buying black slaves in Africa and selling them with great profit in Cuba. The English took Canada instead of America and were sure that something would stop the swarms of humanity to their south moving west, the wilderness or the Indians or the Mississippi River or the French and Spanish territories. We would never reach the west coast and the Pacific Ocean and what kind of government could ever rule and dominate such vast swirls of humanity coming from all over the world and always on the move west in spite of the great overwhelming difficulties? There was so much history to look at and so many contradictions that historians gave us simple themes. Anglo-Saxons were the key. They gave us Anglo-Saxon common law for our courts and the English language and a tradition of political freedom. This at least was true. Historians' simplistic statements gave us the sense that a few basic deeds in our past directly influenced our present and made us Americans. For heroes, George Washington was a true American hero and Abraham Lincoln was not but the lives of both were whittled down to a simplistic shape to provide recognizable figures that inspired national unity. Abraham Lincoln's bad deeds were expunged and the heroic image of Lincoln that reached our history books was worshipful and created national unity. The most extreme simplification was the division historians wrote about that they discovered existing just before the Civil War between the north and south. Men in the south were romantic adventurers living off the sweat of black labor and

pretending to be chivalric noblemen proud of their fine and beauti-
ful sentiments, their honor and their lofty respect for the ladies who
were the object of their aristocratic sentiments. The south was overly
agrarian and bogged down in a way of life emphasizing virtues of the
past. The northerners were industrious entrepreneurs eager to escape
from agrarian toil, open to new technologies, settled wherever possible
in towns and cities near rivers whose power was used to run their factories' machines. Historians went on and on constructing cultural differences between English-speaking Protestant men who north and south
had the same British origins and the same middle-class drive to escape
poverty any way possible using their intelligence and initiative. But the
so-called differences, historians said, had caused the war that Abraham
Lincoln had faced so courageously. He had noted before anyone else
that the "house" was "divided". It was not his fault the war. The southerners were a people apart, rebels who had seceded from the union and
were about to attack him and break up the perpetual union. He had
reached deep within himself Lincoln, endured terrible years of war and
suffering but his biblical inspiration and his prophetic knowledge of the
nation's future where there would be "a new burst of freedom" gave him
the spiritual strength to win the war and taught us in our schools the
lesson that we Americans could endure anything and achieve anything
if we succeeded in incorporating in ourselves President Lincoln's heroic
character. He had bequeathed to us an America glorious and free. We
were on our own in his new nation but he had left us by his courageous
individual actions a model of how to succeeded on our own.

We were taught that the Constitution had formed the nation but this
was only partly true because it had set up a Federal Government and
also divided sovereign power between the Federal Government and the
states. The real genius of the Constitution remained hidden from us. It
had not only divided sovereignty but also had made a clear judgment
about the relationship between sovereignty and democracy. Democracy
does not require full sovereignty according to the Constitution because
it sets up a federal democratic government without granting the Federal
Government full sovereignty. It takes some sovereign powers from the
states and transfers them to the Federal Government but in turn in

Article IV Section 4. it is written that "The United States shall guarantee to every State in this Union a Republican Form of Government..." It is the eternal law of the Constitution that quite apart from the question of sovereignty each government, federal or state, *must* be democratic.

Before the ratification of the Constitution in 1787, each of the thirteen colonies was a fully sovereign state. Its ratification was the first attempt ever made in world history to form a union of sovereign states. The previous form of the union under the Articles of Confederation was a union of sovereign states without the states yielding any of their sovereign power. At the present time, the states in the European Union have reached this stage. The states in the EU have yielded no sovereignty but, just as in America under the Articles of Confederation, there is no central government with real sovereign powers. In both cases, the experience of the first stages of an attempt to create a union of sovereign states reveals that there is no real union unless a central government can act with some specified real sovereign powers. Naturally states fear yielding such powers but they then begin to reason about whether or not full sovereignty is necessary in a union of states if states retain enough sovereign power to govern public matters within their states without full sovereignty. The American Constitution grants full absolute sovereignty to the Federal Government only for all military and diplomatic activities. Reason told Americans that a state could remain sovereign without these powers and that it was reasonable for the thirteen states to take the gamble to be rid of them for the sake of the larger possibilities of the union. Since states in the new union would no longer be free to make war on each other or to have diplomatic relations, free interstate commerce would naturally develop on a larger scale than among fully sovereign states. To gain this benefit, American states yielded to the new central government the power to regulate commerce among the states. This was the first time that states anywhere in the world ever established by law free interstate commerce and it anticipated all the way back in the eighteenth century the need that exists today in the twenty-first century for free interstate global commerce. Free interstate commerce established in the American union meant it was necessary logically to have also a system of interstate justice. This led to the establishment of the system of federal courts with the Supreme Court at the top with the power to strike down laws on appeal. But the power granted to the central government over interstate commerce and interstate justice was by no means absolute since states regulated their internal commerce and state courts handled most judicial cases. By 1787 thirteen sovereign independent states had passed through the steps logically necessary to any group of states anywhere in the world that desires to create a substantial and real union.

But implicit in this reasoning was the question of how much sovereignty can be yielded or acquired while at the same time retaining for all the governments of the union, federal and state, democracy. It is implicit in the words of the Constitution that the founding fathers who signed it and the Americans from the states who ratified it believed that a government can be democratic without being fully sovereign. Of course a government of a state that has yielded all military power to a central government can not be a vital democracy unless it is completely free of any threat of invasion by a foreign state. This is the reason that in the sentence in Article IV section 4 of the Constitution that orders the Federal Government to guarantee democracy to every state in the union, it also orders it to protect each state from invasion. The sentence reads: "The United States shall guarantee to every State in this Union a Republican Form of government, and shall protect each of them against Invasion."

From 1861 to 1865 groups of American states made war on one another. The states lost sovereignty but they had already lost sovereignty by ratifying the Constitution and it can be reasonably argued that they were acting before the Civil War with a degree of sovereignty that they no longer possessed. The Federal Government gained sovereignty by starting and winning an unjust war but it can also be reasonably argued that with the union expanding across a continent and adding new states, the central government needed more sovereignty. It as even perhaps reasonable, given its increased continentwide and worldwide responsibilities, to look upon Washington as the national government of a nation among other nations. The states before the Civil War had already proved that the Constitution was correct in assuming that full sovereignty was not necessary to have democracy. But as the Federal Government gained power, democratic governments in states were forced again and again to lose some democratic power by Supreme Court decisions against state laws. Democracy could survive without full sovereignty but at some point the degree of sovereignty of a state must be large enough to equal the degree of it's democratic power and if the degree of sovereignty is not large enough democracy can die. The fight for sovereignty between the federal government and the states could go back and forth from one side to the other as long as the genius of the Constitution prevented the fight from ever killing democracy in any government.

Supreme Court decisions against state laws were not absolutely bad for state democratic governments because they freed business corporations from excessive state regulations and they sometimes asserted the rights of individuals that were universal rights that any state anywhere in the world should not take away from individuals. Absolute democracy as it existed in ancient Athens was dangerous for citizens who were sometimes exiled for opposing democratic decisions. The flagrant power-grabbing that increased political power for radical Republicans by the 14th amendment also produced rights for citizens against democratic states that helped preserve democratic practices. *Some* of the new jurisdiction gained by Congress and the Supreme Court by the 14th amendment destroyed certain powers in sovereign states that might have made them tyrannical by depriving their citizens of universal rights that are due to any citizen of any and every sovereign state. Congress and the Supreme Court certainly used the "due process" clause and the "equal protection of the laws" clause of the 14th amendment to enable all kinds of money-grubbing using Washington's increased powers and the Supreme Court used the amendment to endow not only freed slaves with personal freedom but also to endow corporations with the same freedom by ruling they had the same status before the law as persons. But money-grubbing and the other uncouth practices of bureaucrats, lobbyists and office holders in Washington aside, the 14th amendment does give the force of law to universal human values necessary for human happiness that should be compulsory in any sovereign state whatever located anywhere in the world. What if Washington discovered a radical new useful and far-reaching truth by enacting the 14th amendment that went far beyond the picayune radicalism of the pedestrian radical Republicans: democracy can exist truly and permanently in any sovereign state anywhere in the world only if certain universal human rights, like those embodied in the 13th and 14th amendments and also outlined in the Declaration of Independence and in the Constitution, are forced on states with the force of law by a supranational government whose jurisdiction is constituted not to rule states but instead to force sovereign states to govern justly and democratically?

In the midst of the Civil War, no one thought of such glorious new possibilities for democracy that might come about following the war but Abraham Lincoln did. He spoke in his Gettysburg Address of "a new nation" and of "the great task remaining before us". He said that the men who fought on the fields of Gettysburg had "advanced" an "unfinished work". He said that the "honored dead" should inspire the living to "take increased devotion to that cause for which they gave the last full measure of devotion". What was the cause for which the dead had given "the last full measure of devotion"? It was "that this nation, under God, shall have a new birth of freedom — and that government of the people, by the people, for the people, shall not perish from the earth."

But how could there be "a new birth of freedom" and a government "of the people, by the people, for the people" if Washington continued to use its power to gain more power for itself? The glorious "new birth of freedom" could arrive on the political battlefield only if events in the world forced Washington to stop opposing and start supporting enough sovereignty in its democratic states to allow "a new birth of freedom". Washington itself enjoyed "a new birth of freedom" but Lincoln wanted it not to "perish from the earth". Washington D.C. was but a small dot on the earth. The several states were big blotches and that was where the people lived. Democracy in American states survived the Civil War but some new antithesis to Washington's power would have to rise up in history to force self-alienation and self-regimentation on Washington if governments on "the earth" were ever to be truly "of the people, by the people, for the people".

7

B y the time of the Spanish-American War in 1898, 45 states were
in the union. After the Civil War eleven new states had joined
the union and had duplicated the judicial systems and democratic governments of their sister states. A vast revolutionary economic
development unlike anything in the rest of the world roared ahead sav-
agely with little governmental restraint across a continent. Yet the world
within the united states and the world outside seemed completely indifferent to the political revolution that was also going on. Americans concentrated on succeeding in the workplace and they had little interest in
any of their governments, federal or state, because they knew they did
little directly for their economic benefit. But it was nonetheless the radical new political system that made economic success for more and more
people possible. Wealth was bountiful in America but the existence
across a continent of 45 states with elected governors and elected leg-
islatures in democratic assemblies was also bountiful. Washington had
the power granted in the Constitution to regulate commerce among
the states. This meant that no state could close its borders to interstate
commerce. The Supreme Court used the 14th amendment again and
again in judgments in favor of corporations to assure their freedom to
do business in states without excessive state regulation. Industry roared
ahead creating radical new wealth precisely because businesses operated in a political system where no government was fully sovereign and

every one was democratic and therefore open to control by anyone at all. Corporations and political parties and individuals fought to pass through countless doors open to political power. Interlocking networks of corporations developed to a degree that was simply astounding putting control of the corporate part of the American economy in the hands of a small number of men. People worldwide read about the bounteous economic expansion in America with awe. Of those who noted the expansion in America of the states to 45, few reacted to it with appropriate awe. The 45 states all had democratic governments and their governments created for their citizens the same civilized public necessities that other states in the world created for their citizens. The difference was that foreign states worldwide were fully sovereign and rarely democratic. 45 American states knew that they would never be fully sovereign and they were learning under the domination of Washington that their limited sovereignty did not mean that they could not fully enjoy democratic state governments. America was experiencing Lincoln's "new burst of freedom" in hundreds of different centers of democratic power made possible precisely because it was a union of democratic states held together and forced to govern democratically by a democratic central government.

America in 1898 was nothing less than a model for the future political organization of the world. America had established a continental union of states and the central government of the union, even with its increased national power, was not a fully sovereign government except over the military and diplomacy. The 13 original states had gambled that they could remain free without the power to make war. From the beginning, Washington had used its war power offensively. It had started wars in 1812 with England and in 1846 with Mexico. Then with 34 states in the union Lincoln had used his war power against 11 American states. The Civil War shocked and stunned the people of the states north and south yet only a few brave voices had openly condemned Lincoln's use of the federal war power against Americans. Certainly the men from Virginia and other southern states who helped write the Constitution had never imagined that the exclusive war power they granted Washington could be used against themselves. A kind of political quiet reigned after the war. People did not want to talk about it. The real political doings in Washington became a touchy subject. People knew that politicians whispered to one another in corridors making deals on the sly but they preferred that politicians whispered so that they could not be heard clearly. The only sounds that Americans enjoyed hearing in this blank time of savage industrial development were the noises of their work and those of immigrants who could not speak English working in their factories.

But even an aloof and imperial Washington secure in its national power was forever in need of more power. It could sit back at home and let things go on around it freely or else interfere but interference was an indirect usage of its power and its war power could be used directly. Looking back at the America of 1898, it is extremely difficult to understand how no observers saw the danger for the world. How could anyone at home in America or foreigners abroad not observe that a central government with no national territory located in a federal district possessed dominant political power over 45 states? Why was it not evident that a new Rome had arisen in Washington that in the Civil War had amassed a huge land army and had conquered for itself national and imperial power? It had no national territory Washington but it did not need any if it had the constitutional right and the means to declare war on whomever it wished whenever it wished. No one in the 45 American states, no one in the nation-states and empires on earth had any power at all to take away the absolute power to make war at will possessed by Washington. No doubt foreigners comforted themselves with the idea that America was just another nation among nations and that they all had the power to make war. It was no big deal. Washington had 45 states supporting it with state territories sometimes larger than most states on earth. That was no big deal either. Millions and millions of immigrants were filling American states year after year avid to join America's roaring industrial revolution. It was a big deal for Washington. Washington without any national territory had to show from time to time its own states and the states of the world that its war power made it just as much a national power without national territory as the nations with national territory that it decided to fight. This meant that the Federal Government would inevitably play both a national and international role. Its national role had its origins in continental developments among American states. Its international role would grow because the free economic development that it supported in America was so successful that it would be impossible to confine it to American states.

McKinley, the American president in 1898, did not start the war with Spain for any particular reason that made the war necessary. Theodore Roosevelt, who became president in 1902, wrote a friend in 1897, "In strict confidence...I should welcome almost any war, for I think this country needs one." Voices were raised in America loudly against the war but it seemed no more than a clumsy entrance of America into the ranks of the European imperialists who were colonizing weaker peoples all over the earth. The Federal Government had carved out for itself the national role of governing mainly by interfering in the operations of American state governments. But it had already transferred its field of operations to worldwide interventions and by 1895 had also interfered in the affaires of countries 103 times urged on by the fact that it had not only exclusive war power but also exclusive diplomatic power. By this time, it had used military force against Argentina, Nicaragua, Japan, Uruguay, Angola, China and Hawaii. The war with Spain was its first entrance into the regular ranks of imperialist nations because it won for itself from Spain control of Cuba, the Philippines, and Puerto Rico. But European-style imperialism was not for Washington. It handled its control of Cuba and the Philippines badly. It released them from its political control as quickly as possible and contented itself with being free to interfere with them internally either diplomatically or militarily whenever necessary. Many condemned the United States war with Spain as an imperialist adventure, but few asked the deeper question of whether or not it had been wise to grant Washington in the Constitution absolute diplomatic and war powers. Could anyone in Washington control such powers? What would be the consequences for the world of the future in the twentieth century if Washington with a rapidly expanding union of states about to reach 48 could use its enormous power to gain entrance for its hands into the internal affaires not only of its own states but of any state? Anyone who asked such a question surely would ask it fearing that Washington's interference in the internal affaires of states could only be bad. It's interference in its own states' business had not always been bad and sometimes had been very good. But the possible good actions of any state never entered into thoughts about a state's actions in a time of rough and ready worldwide imperialism and anyone in diplomatic circles would have been openly laughed at who even suggested that Washington's power might one day be used *for the good of the world.* Washington at the time of the Spanish-American war was considered no more than a new junior member of the imperialist gang.

Woodrow Wilson, a democrat elected president in 1912, actively and passionately thought about using American power for worldwide good. He shared the pacifist and progressive views of nineteenth-century reformers like LaFolette and William Jennings Bryan who became his Secretary of State. Many Americans believed idealistically that America despite setbacks was rushing towards some wonderful new happy future and that America would somehow be able to transfer this glorious future to the rest of humanity. Mark Twain wrote of "the drive, and push, and rush and struggle of the raging, tearing, booming nineteenth century" but many theories abounded during the period claiming that at the end of the dark tunnel would be the light of Progress with a capital P. American soldiers and diplomats had treated the people of Cuba and the Philippines badly and denied them freedom and democracy but some even believed that such crude and inhuman treatment had a positive and civilizing effect. President Wilson sent American soldiers into Mexico to interfere in its internal politics but even this did not darken his view of the light American power could shed over darkness and when war broke out in Europe in 1914, he worked as forcefully as he could to keep America out of it. Instead of rushing into the war on the side of England and France against Germany, he stuck to his pacifist principles and using American diplomatic channels, he tried to get the three powers to negotiate an end to the war rather than to continue fighting. Theodore Roosevelt, a former president and a hero of the Spanish-American war, despised Wilson's pacifist approach and wanted war. So did many influential men and Wilson risked being considered a coward. But the people loved him. They wanted as passionately as he to stay out of the war. He was an American president who did not jump at the chance to use his war power. A former professor of History, Wilson understood that if America entered full-scale the war in Europe, it would cause a profound change in America. For one thing, the millions of new immigrants from various European nationalities had never been urged to become Americans. They had instead been encouraged to keep their national identity and create for themselves national associations and newspapers in their native languages. When the German navy's submarine warfare became intolerable and forced Wilson to declare war on Germany in 1917, he knew he had to use the Federal Government to try to shape America into a nation. "It is not an army that we must train and shape for war. It is a nation," he wrote in his draft proclamation. "The whole nation must be a team." But his practical task of nation-building did not preclude in his mind the necessity of America being at the same time a force in the world for good. He said as part of a speech he gave for a Liberty Load Drive in Baltimore on April 6 1918, "Force, Force to the utmost, Force without stint or limit, the righteous and triumphant Force which shall make Right the law of the world, and cast every selfish dominion down in the dust."

On the January 8 1918, 10 months before the end of the war, Wilson argued before Congress that he was fighting the war for a moral purpose and he outlined 14 points that he believed if accepted by belligerents and others would bring about a just peace and a world oriented towards goodness. In his 14 points, he tried to find a balance between nationalism and internationalism. Two of his points called for open covenants in dealings between nations and freedom of the seas. Ten gave specific details setting up borders and territories for national states and argued for the free development of peoples enclosed within empires towards national states. Only two of the points referred to a new internationalism. Point 3 called for, "The removal of all economic barriers and the establishment of equality of trade conditions among all the nations consenting to the peace and associating themselves for its maintenance." Point 14 said, "A general association of nations must be formed under specific covenants for the purpose of affording mutual guarantees of political independence and territorial integrity to great and small states alike."

Point 3 and point 14, even though among points designed to establish international peace, are none the less in broad outline a sketch of the political principals of the American union of states. The American states by consenting to the Constitution certainly assented to point 3 because by giving their central government control over interstate commerce they had removed "all economic barriers" between their states and established "equality of trade conditions" not "among all the nations" but among all the states, who had the right according to the Declaration of Independence to be "separate and independent states". And of course as united American states they had already consented to what president Wilson wanted the nations of the world of 1918 to consent to by "consenting to the peace and associating themselves for its maintenance" because the American states had united more than a hundred years before to maintain among themselves peace. Point 14 said, "A general association of nations must be formed under specific covenants for the purpose of affording mutual guarantees of political independence and territorial integrity to great and small states alike". The United States of America had certainly already done that too because by adopting the Constitution the states agreed to establish by law "mutual guarantees of political independence and territorial integrity to great and small states alike". Wilson was imagining a united states of the world for the nations of the world using his own United States of America as a general model.

Aritcle IV, section 3. of the American Constitution says, "New States may be admitted by the Congress into this Union." In Paris for talks in 1919 after the war, President Wilson was approached by groups seeking his aid to help establish for their people the status of independent sovereign states, people like the Irish or the Serbs who suffered under imperial controls. President Wilson could have invited any and all peoples he met with, both those already living in states and those about to achieve statehood, to apply to his Congress in Washington D.C. to be admitted to his union of states which already had in operation points 3 and 14 of his 14 points. If he had done so and if European states had applied to Congress and been admitted to the United States of America, the name of our union could conveniently have been changed to "The United States of America and Europe" or, since states outside of Europe might have also applied for admission to Congress, a more suitable new name might have been simply, "The United States of the World."

Europeans before the war had seen clearly the danger of crowding together on their continent nation-states and empires building up their military strength behind borders and ready to break out and pounce on one another. But they could not envision how a "United States of Europe" could take form. Each state and empire had their own independent economy at work separated from one another and selfishly protected by tariffs. Socialism was the hope of many Europeans because it seemed to be an economic system that could possibly be applied universally while capitalism was narrowly confined behind national borders and used foreign colonies for outlets for surplus manufactures. Also the nation-state seemed essential to democracy because any type of limited sovereignty in a state seemed to mean a state would be under an alien rule and therefore could not have a democratic government. If President Wilson had boldly proposed that all the states of the world apply to Congress for admission to his American union and that it become a "United States of the World" with Washington transforming itself from a national government to a supranational world central government, other major difficulties would have been that at the time there was no worldwide economic system and many parts of the earth had no states at all but instead were colonial territories.

Wilson's 14 points were a public statement of a United States foreign policy that would continue for the twentieth century. The policy had an inherent contradiction. On the one hand in 10 of his points Wilson argued for both the continued existence of national states already existing such as Germany, Russia, Belgium, Italy and France and for the emergence as national states of territories or empires such as Poland, Serbia, Montenegro and Turkey. He used very assertive language in these 10 points to either strengthen or create national states and then, on the other hand, in point 14, he wanted a "general association of nations" with "specific covenants" for "affording mutual guarantees of political independence and territorial integrity to great and small states alike". He wanted to give existing nation-states and emerging nation-states each of them total absolute sovereignty which means their right to do among other nation-states whatever their power might allow them to do and at the same time he wanted to restrict their power to interrupt the peace of the world by agreeing to "covenants" to protect internationally "great and small states alike". He wanted nation-states to continue to exist or come into existence and then agree not to act like nation-states. He wanted nation-states to have sovereignty and also agree to limit it. He wanted the states of the world to agree to something like the limited sovereignty that the American Constitution allowed the sovereign states of America. Wilson wanted the war that American soldiers had helped win in France to produce sovereign nation-states all over Europe with newly drawn borders and avoid any future war by agreeing to "covenants". He wanted the states of Europe to have the power to wage war and at the same time agree not to use the power.

President Wilson went to the peace conference in 1919 and proposed a means to unite the states of Europe and the world. His proposal for a League of Nations was the first airy and idealistic attempt to produce a united states of the world. His league of nations failed for the simple reason that a "nation" and "full-sovereignty" are synonymous and one "full-sovereignty" can not unite with another "full-sovereignty". It is like trying to make a marriage of two people who do not agree in advance to sacrifice their freedom. The American experience of attempting to unite sovereign states has proved that no substantial union of states is possible unless states agree to limit their sovereignty. The American experience also proved that states with limited sovereignty can survive even a civil war still sovereign and can continue to be flourishing democracies provided universal human rights are guaranteed to all citizens of a union in a written constitution and individual rights are protected and reinforced by decisions of federal courts. Wilson's point 3 called for "The removal of all economic barriers and the establishment of equality of trade conditions among all the nations…". Free trade worldwide was necessary for the happiness of the world and its peoples. The American experience of free trade among its 45 united states proved that a union of states with limited sovereignty could produce massive and universal wealth. But world trade presently was going on in spite of nations and it could never be totally free unless nations could be convinced to limit their sovereignty by joining a worldwide union of states. Regular sovereignty worked against free world trade and defended within national borders national economies that restricted the growth of their citizens' wealth. Wilson returned to America after the peace talks in Paris in 1919 and campaigned passionately for his League of Nations. The American Senate voted against it. American diplomats continued nonetheless to work and argue for worldwide peace and worldwide free trade even as they supported the existence of nation-states everywhere and hoped that they would be democratically constituted. Democracy and nation-states after the First World War had difficult marriages and many painful divorces. By the Second World War, the American union had grown to 48 states with limited sovereignty and all enjoyed democratic state governments that controlled 90 percent of the public governmental business of the United States. Democracy worked in America partly because Article IV section 4 of the Constitution forces the Federal Government to produce democracy in its states: "The United States shall guarantee to every State in this Union a Republican Form of Government, and shall protect each of them against Invasion;..." Washington accomplishes this duty by interfering in state governments using the federal judiciary to put corrupt state politicians on trial and put them in jail. Its armed forces protect its democratic states from invasion. The United States works well because it is possible within a union of states with limited sovereignty to embody points 3 and 14 of Wilson's 14 points and create at least in America a league of states that may convince nations worldwide some day to apply to the Congress in Washington for admission as new states to our union and help us establish by loyalty to our Constitution and our written laws a real league of nations, a real united states of the world.

8

I n 1918 the states of the world were far from being united and the economic systems within states risked being transformed in the near future to communist systems. In Russia a communist revolution had taken place and the Tsar's family had been assassinated. The nobles were being expelled from their properties, the middle-class capitalistic economy was being overthrown by socialist revolutionaries, and the working class was rising to the top of the confused heap eager to try to run the economy without allowing individuals to seek wealth by competing with one another. In 1918 President Wilson, with American soldiers now fighting in the trenches in France, no longer cared very much about the war. He let the professional soldiers take care of it and withdrew more and more from public contact thinking deeply about world problems. He was afraid that the revolution that was happening in Russia could happen anywhere. In the United States before the war, anarchists and socialists had been openly threatening the middle-class capitalistic social order. To conduct the war in Europe, he began censoring the press and repressing groups who opposed his policies. New bureaucratic commissions were created in Washington run by businessmen who volunteered their expertise to transform the Federal Government into a spread of agencies ruling either directly or indirectly over industries for the national war effort. Wilson's "nation-building" necessary to train 3,000,000 young Americans for the war in France took forms for governing in Washington that were the beginning of the vast federal apparatus of commissions and bureaus that we know today. The national government was growing bigger and stronger and the war was going well in Europe but President Wilson was still very worried about the world and the form of the world of the future. He confided in his wife's brother, Dr. Stockton Axson, "The next president will have to be able to think in terms of the whole world. He must be internationally minded...the only really internationally minded people are the labor people. They are in touch with world movements." He believed that after the war the world would change radically, that governments would have to take over certain industries, that power sources like coal mines and oilfields would have to be government owned. "If I should say that outside," he exclaimed to Dr. Axson, "people would call me a socialist, but I am not a socialist. And it is because I am not a socialist that I believe these things." At home, radicals were inspired by Bolshevik propaganda against capitalism and Wilson felt a "baneful seething" among the working class and the foreign born that bothered him deeply. He felt that only the government's direct actions in the American economy could prevent communism arising in America. Abroad, he fought the rise of communism in Russia by sending American soldiers to Russia to fight the Bolsheviks.

In 1913, in the second year of Wilson's presidency, his government received two weapons that in the long run eliminated or neutralized threats in America and in the world to the stability and expansion of middle-class capitalism from competing communist or socialist economic systems. Congress passed that year the Revenue Act creating a federal income tax on individual and business income and the Federal Reserve Act creating the Federal Reserve banking system. Wilson died in 1924 and did not see or understand the long-term revolutionary effects these federal laws would have on American states and states worldwide. The Bolshevik seizure of power in Russia has been described as ten days that shook the world. The Revenue Act and the Federal Reserve Act made just slight tremors at first but the tremors grew stronger and then began shaking powerfully. The shaking has never stopped. The Federal Reserve Act empowered private banks to create the public money supply of the United States and the Revenue Act started rivers of money flowing from millions of individuals and businesses to Washington. The Federal Government did not have to take over industries as Wilson thought to save capitalism. The income tax law made the Federal Government the largest richest most powerful corporation that has ever existed or can exist on the face of the earth and the new banking system that was established by law freed individuals and corporations to finance their economic ventures so easily and so profitably that they were able to send an ever increasing supply of money to Washington.

The 16th amendment to the Constitution of 1913 establishing the federal income tax and the new radical banking system established by the Federal Reserve Act produced a mighty torrent of monies flowing in many thousands of different directions in vast rivers watering and fertilizing vital ingenious enterprises in a flood of economic activity so overwhelming that, a hundred years later, today, the American economy is still a wonder on earth. Federal taxes on income and profits sent money to Washington and the freedom of private banks to create all the public money of 48 states as they saw fit set the American economy afloat on a flood of rivers of money overflowing their banks and creating new waters of opportunity everywhere. New rivers of economic opportunity kept rising up overflowing and swelling the flood for millions and millions of free citizens in a huge union of united states.

In Russia in 1921, the Bolsheviks created not thousands of banks to create locally where it was needed capital for individual economic ventures but instead one central bank, Gosbank, to impose centralized control on all industries. The central bank provided monies from on top downwards to favored individuals and enterprises wherever it saw fit without considering whether or not they were creditworthy as did middle-class capitalist bankers. The bank dictated from on high what economic activity was allowed. It did not act at all as a commercial bank and used the bank balances it allowed enterprises not to free them to pursue their individual goals but to monitor whether or not they complied with the five-year plan set for them by the Gosbank. This top-down approach of the central communist bank was a kind of bad imitation of top-down central banks in operation in middle-class run economies in

European nation-states. The capitalistic central banks were top-down too. Some of them, like the Bank of England, even at one time had the power to create all the money in the English economy. The other bad banking method that was used in Europe was regulating the supply of money by relating its value to the value of gold deposits held in banks. This did little more than put a stupid brake on economic development and the English central bank by controlling the value of English money also influenced negatively the money supply in Europe and America. William Jennings Bryant, running as a Democrat for president in 1896, had used strong American sentiment against conservative banking practices for the main issue of his campaign. He railed against the repressive effect of England's banking practice that maintained gold as the standard for controlling the value of money which in turn regulated the total supply of money. The gold standard was crippling the American economy. Bryant exclaimed at the end of his speech arguing for a radically increased money supply in America, "You shall not press down upon the brow of labor this crown of thorns, you shall not crucify mankind upon a cross of gold." Gosbank in Russia pressed down a crown of thorns on Russia's economy for more than half a century. As the twentieth century progressed, European central banks did find ways despite their top-down approach to free their commercial banks to increase their supplies of money using creative banking practices, but none of them reached the scope and the level of freedom that the Federal Reserve Act legally granted private banks in the American union.

From the foundation of the Federal Government, some wanted a central bank in Washington that could control top-down America's money supply as in European states. William Jennings Bryant and the progressives wanted a central bank under public control. This would have meant the direct control of banks in all the states by the Federal Government. But since the Civil War, the Federal Government had not opted for direct control of state governments but rather for interference. It opted to remain back and above most government functions as a referee ready always to insert itself where necessary to settle disputes and decide what was valid universally. But from the beginning bankers like state political leaders had been operating independently of Washington creating money for local enterprises just as state political leaders had been creating laws independently for their states. Most of the bankers were against federal-government intervention in the banks by political appointees in Washington. The Federal Reserve system of 1913 was a hybrid system, both public and private, both centralized and decentralized. It allowed private bankers unheard-of freedom to create money and it provided strong but very limited central control. Its structure is unique among central banking systems very much as the centralized-decentralized structure of the government of the United States is unique among nations and radically different from nation-states. Regional Federal Reserve banks are set up in major US cities and private banks elect their boards of directors. Boards of Governors of the overall system are selected by the President and confirmed by Congress, but they make decisions to support private bankers independently of the US government and they are self-financed. The whole system is set up just as though the Federal Government wished to have as little to do as possible with the nation's money supply. The Federal Reserve system is simply astounding. Private banks invest deposits they receive from customers in an account with a Federal Reserve bank and create multiples of money through loans to businesses sometimes 900 percent greater than the value of their deposits. Bankers throughout the history of America created money for whomever and for whatever largely as they individually saw fit and now these revolutionary banking practices were solidified legally in a system independent of any government. The Treasury Department of the United States prints money but this is not creation of money. Printed money is simply made available to member banks when they need it to give to their customers who prefer printed money in hand rather than an account in their bank. The real money supply exists as accounts in banks and money is transferred largely by checks. Banks can not be chartered in Washington D.C. and must be chartered in one of the states. If the creation of money is the main tool of a democratic government, then in this case the states rule supremely and the Federal Government is but a marginal player relegated to the sidelines. Banks are free either to join the Federal Reserve system or not. Customers of those who join make deposits that are insured up to a certain sum by the Federal Government. The economic enterprises in any state need money to be born and more money to live. Creating money creates enterprises. The Federal Government has decided once and for all by federal law that enterprises in its union of states will be free enterprises.

A tax on individual and business income is normal in a normal state but the Federal Government of the United States is not set up by the Constitution as a state and the 16th amendment authorizing such taxes to be sent to it created another monetary revolution. Washington interferes with state governments when it desires to challenge state authority or when the Constitution or decisions against state laws by the Supreme Court give it authority to act. It must fund its military and its diplomatic corps because only here is its national authority exclusive. Congress under the Constitution has power to govern interstate commerce and as the twentieth century progressed, the Supreme Court judged that just about any activity in a state could be construed as interstate commerce. This gave Congress near universal authority over commerce but it did not compel it to act to regulate commerce in a manner that would require it to fund with federal tax monies what commerce it chose to regulate. Primary, secondary and university education could be construed as interstate commerce and could therefore be regulated and funded by Congress. If so, this would be an example of an action normal in any state. A state collects income taxes and in turn finances public projects in its state that must be handled universally for the public good. In the United States political system, the Federal Government decides the uses of its tax monies and there are so many states with such varied needs that it is difficult and sometimes impossible to allocate federal funds universally for one specific public need. Washington therefore uses its income taxes to fund projects that its discretion deems worthy and that are not necessarily in the public interest. Even when Congress allocates tax monies to govern it does not govern directly within states but instead sets up departments and bureaus located both in Washington and in states that govern indirectly and from the outside with limited authority. The Federal Department of Education, for example, does not fund or rule education but instead creates studies or projects that may or may not be adopted and used by state education departments. The Federal Government granted itself a police power not granted in the Constitution by establishing and funding the Federal Bureau of Investigation, the FBI, which aids police departments in states but the states fund and manage about 95 percent of all police activity in the union. The Federal Government's discretion has created many federal departments to operate indirectly in the states' business of governing and this means in practice that pools of money are sent regularly to Washington for Congress to use however it chooses and wherever it chooses, either nationally or internationally. Section 4. of the 14th amendment to the Constitution states, "The validity of the public debt of the United States, authorized by law, including debts incurred for payment of pensions and bounties for services in suppressing insurrection or rebellion, shall not be questioned." Before the Civil War, the Washington government had great difficulties financing its limited activities but the 14th amendment increased its revenues greatly and the new Income Tax law of 1913 gave it the legs and the pockets full of money to go where it wanted and do whatever it wanted. Washington became the world's biggest spender and except in its military operations, there was very little it did with its money that was not good, sometimes very good, both for the world's states and empires and for its own states.

In the fourth century AD, Saint Augustine in his great book, *The City of God*, the *Civitas Dei*, claims that in world history two states exist side by side, the *civitas dei* and the *civitas terrena*, the heavenly city of God composed of the good and the earthly city composed of the unredeemed. Humans either live in one city or the other according to whether they direct themselves towards the love of God or the love of themselves. Eventually at the end of history the two states will be separated at the last judgment. Is it possible that Washington as world history develops in the twenty-first century might evolve and become a central world international government and a worldwide champion promoting Augustine's *civitas dei*? Is it possible that Washington could transcend completely the lowly tasks of the *civitas terrena* and become a powerful force promoting justice, civil decency and democratic freedoms universally?

Peoples in the past have created communities inspired by their view of the divine. Ancient Egypt was a divine empire. Every human being was considered divine even though only one, the pharaoh, could be raised beyond the human-divine to the level of the cosmic-divine. It was holy work for humans to build superhuman pyramids, temples and statues that reaffirmed for eternity both the pharaoh's eminence and their own. Moses and the Israelites escaped the Egyptian empire and created instead a small community where the divine could live in an arc or a temple as a living presence. Ancient philosophers believed the business of governing was a divine vocation. Moses' laws for his community taught that only moral goodness could open the door from the divine presence in temples to the divine presence in the human soul. Crossing the Red Sea and the Sinai desert to ancient Israel was a transition from an empire to a nation-state, the first known to history, that was at the same time both a political and religious revolution. The Romans, who considered themselves divine through their ancestor Aeneas' mother Venus, allowed some democratic freedom in the city-states established throughout their empire. Rome filled its cities with magnificent temples and buildings and god-like statues of humans. A human who walked through Imperial Rome felt himself in a *civitas dei* but Saint Augustine in his book describes so extensively the immorality of the gods who were adored in Roman temples that there could be no doubt but that Rome was in reality a *civitas terrena* and its resemblance to a heavenly city but an illusion. The poet Ovid took the same position as Augustine for he proclaimed in his book *The Art of Love* that the goddess Venus was the fostering divinity of Rome and her city, Rome, the greatest place on earth to find and seduce women. The Emperor Augustus expected Romans to emulate the magnificence of Rome by the magnificence of their moral conduct and he rewarded Ovid's manner of worshiping Venus with permanent exile from her favorite city. The Emperor at least believed that Roman behavior should resemble the divine and that the semblance that resulted would make mere humans super humans.

The German philosopher Hegel wrote the greatest work examining humanity's progress towards the expression of the divine in history. He does not write of God or of the city of God and examines instead the development and progress in world history of what he calls "universal spirit". This rationalized spirit expresses itself throughout history in a variety of finite forms all of which fail to reveal the universal spirit absolutely. Each finite and imperfect form of universal spirit is inevitably surpassed in a dialectical movement by a new finite form which reaches a higher form although still finite. In Hegel's *Philosophy of History* he identifies the progress of the world towards universal spirit as progress towards freedom. The oriental world, he writes, knew only the freedom of one man, as the pharaoh in Egypt. The Greek and Roman world knew the freedom only of some men, since slavery was instituted. The Protestant Germanic states of Hegel's time, the early nineteenth century, finally realize the freedom of all. "The essential being," he wrote, "is the union of the subjective with the rational will: it is the moral whole, the state, which is that form of reality in which the individual has and enjoys his freedom".

The greatest political creation of middle-class revolutionaries in Europe was the nation-state and Hegel is correct that, at least for the middle class, it was the form of reality in which they enjoyed their freedom. The states in Europe by the nineteenth century existed mainly to allow middle-class lawyers to write laws securing the properties and riches of the middle class and for the most part exempting the rich from taxes. Hegel did not wish to see what might develop in the future world beyond the European world of his time which was coalescing into the universality of nation-states. He did declare however that, "America is therefore the land of the future where in the ages that lie before us, the burden of the world's history shall reveal itself." These prophetic words give us no notion of what form the new revelation will take. To discover the new form that may be possible, we must go back and discover the deficiencies of previous peoples.

The ancient Greeks failed to create a lasting empire because they could not extend citizenship universally. The Romans expanded citizenship greatly but not universally and the form of limited sovereignty that they allowed their subjects was the government of the city-state, the local *civitas terrena*, not the nation-state. The British Empire matched the greatness of Rome but it created a world union of colonies and could not free itself from the need to dominate and rule peoples. Neither Rome nor London discovered that transferring some of their central power not to a union of city-states or colonies but to a union of states with real sovereign powers in each state was the essential key to maintaining their own power. Washington universalized citizenship, universalized the American states' sovereign powers, and when it finally, after years of struggle pro and con, gave the power of creating money to individually owned or incorporated state banks, the burden of the world's history that Hegel wrote about seemed to be finally becoming unburdened.

In 1913 America also took the other revolutionary step necessary to begin unburdening itself. Rome and London found that financing themselves with tax monies from their subjects became more and more difficult as their empires grew. Rome had to commission tax collectors at exorbitant rates to go all over forcing money from hundreds of diverse peoples living in poverty. London lost a large portion of its empire by trying to impose taxes on Americans. Washington in 1913 coolly created the 16th Amendment to the Constitution universalizing a tax on income. Every individual or business had now to send a portion of their income or their profit to Washington. Hegel's "universal spirit" found a home in Washington D.C. because the federal income tax gave federal politicians the freedom to act as universally as they wished and to fund both their good and bad ventures lavishly. Washington had not acted tyrannically after the Civil War as Abraham Lincoln had acted and as they could have acted. Politicians who flocked there, elected by state voters, discovered that the burden of history was light as long as they acted universally. Washington found the key to free itself from being imprisoned in a *civitas terrena* chained to the drudgery of national rule. Let the states rule! Let everyone born in any state have citizenship in the US and also in the state where they choose to live! Two citizenships are better than one! Let everyone be free to work and live and create wherever they will! But let every worker and every businessman send a portion of their earnings to Washington and let them not demand their contributions back! Washington learned to rule as little as possible and the citizens and the businesses of states learned not to demand back from Washington their monies. Every citizen learned he was on his own to either make it or not according to the degree of initiative and energy he could devise. Washington learned it was on its own too and it found that the safest way to keep the rivers of money flowing to it was to act as universally as possible. It found, as the twentieth century developed and world history burdened it with worldwide commitments, that even in areas where the Constitution demanded that it govern, that is, in military, diplomatic and commercial matters, even here it could pursue universal ends. No one can rationally argue that the worldwide commercial, military and diplomatic activities of Washington for the second half of the twentieth century were undertaken for purely national objectives. Washington's diplomats routinely pursued goals of democracy and freedom for foreign nations globally and American corporations were soon producing more goods and services outside the US than inside. Washington learned to use the national powers granted it by the Constitution universally. Even the large sums of money that Washington borrows from rich foreigners have a universal aspect. Most of the money comes from foreign banks. Washington's largess bankrolls bankers globally by paying them guaranteed interest on their money. Washington alone of national governments has experienced the divine sweetness of acting as little as possible as the government of a nation. It wills what it wishes and it has learned that if it wills only what the United States of America wish, it will no longer be doing the work of Hegel's "universal spirit" and it will no longer provide a stage where federal politicians possess the resources to act like the saintly members of Saint Augustine's *civitas dei*

9

Now, at the beginning years of the twenty-first century, a real united states of the world is necessary and a real political system already in operation exists for creating such a world union of states. A worldwide interplay of economic activities originating all over our globe in various states has created a global economy that can not develop to its full potential unless real democracy and positive economic development for all citizens of all nations in the world at all levels of the economic ladder can be guaranteed by law. After the First World War, peoples in Europe and elsewhere rushed avidly to create nation-states for themselves. After the Second World War, peoples in former European colonies found themselves in new nation-states with borders drawn for them by their former European rulers. Meanwhile, after the First World War, the globalization of the world's economy began and took steps both forward and back. After the Second World War, globalization struggled through the Cold War to finally race forward after the defeat of communism to the astounding worldwide economic development we know today. States both large and small, both powerful and weak, tried as best they could to deal with world wars and globalization but none of them, even the powerful, have been successful to the degree that would have been possible if they had been states joined to one another in a union of states. President Wilson set up such a union in 1919 in his League of Nations and failed to convince US politicians to join his league. The

French had a plan at the time for setting up a supranational congress for the permanent pacification of the world and the English had a plan for a Commonwealth of Nations. Both plans came to nothing. No one dared throughout the twentieth century to ask nation-states to limit their sovereignty and assign the bits of sovereignty they gave up to a supranational government in a city that was not located within any state. No one dared to offer such states in exchange for agreeing to accept limited sovereignty democratic participation in the business of the supranational government by sending elected representatives from their states to the supranational congress of the new union of states. The United States of America already has such a union in operation. The Congress of the United States has the right stated in the Constitution to admit new states. Every state in the world that applies to the Congress and is admitted will take a step towards a democratic government guaranteed to its state by law and towards revolutionary economic development using advanced economic laws like the Federal Reserve Act to create modern banks. Every such state will be free forever from the tyranny of corrupt government officials in their state because the average citizen will be protected by a supranational judiciary system and every state will be free from civil and external wars protected by a supranational military. The states of the United States are already democratic states members of a fifty-state interstate union. Democratic government is so strong in American states that it survived even a disastrous Civil War. The United States of America *must* become The United States of the World to create the just and good world of the future that humanity needs and deserves.

President Wilson, exhausted and sick, traveled by train all over the United States in 1919 wearing himself out making speech after speech to try to gain popular support for his League of Nations. He knew that the senate in Washington was against it. He tried to gain enough favor by appealing directly to the public so that the senate would be forced to ratify the treaty of Versailles. He knew as did other world leaders that there would be another world war, worse than the First World War, if no worldwide global force was set up to pacify warlike nation-states. He tried to make Americans begin to think globally. They listened to his passionate speeches patiently and sometimes enthusiastically, but

Americans wanted nothing to do with globalization. They did not even know what it was globalization. The American congress had admitted two new states as recently as 1912, Arizona and New Mexico, states with combined territories larger than France. 48 states spread across a continent were globalization enough for Americans. They did not need any more of the world. They had plenty already. The Senate voted against ratification of the treaty of Versailles. President Wilson died in 1924 having given his all to set up in a preliminary form a united states of the world.

The world of independent national states settled itself back behind various national borders and the 1920s saw some fast national economic developments. Americans were one hundred percent nationalistic too but practically speaking they cared little about their nation, still less about globalization, and just enjoyed their postwar economic boom. The opportunities available to become wealthy were magical. American banks with their radical new powers pumped out money as though it were free and unlimited water from some secret well. A European clerk could save enough money to book an Atlantic passage in steerage and off the ship in New York he could make a week's pay at three times what he earned in Europe. America had 48 states and no borders that were barriers to interstate trade and to the free passage to any state of its people. You could go where you wanted. You could try your luck anywhere. An American already had a global reach for his interests within 48 states stretched across a continent and his government in Washington was doing little or nothing to govern him or his adventures.

The First World War made everyone in America an American. There was no doubt any longer but that the sons and daughters of recent European immigrants were Americans too. America had fought a war allied to great nations and against great nations and had proved to the world that it was a great nation too. The descendants of the Anglo-Saxons who had immigrated to America before the more recent immigrants went along with the new nationalism but they still were firmly against the Federal Government and all other American governments. They were loyal citizens like everyone else and they accepted of course that governments were necessary. But they wanted as little to do with any government as possible and they believed like a holy law written in stone that anyone who expected any aid in any form from American governments was a degenerate. Work made an American an American. Work and nothing else. There was plenty of work and plenty of money. Immigrants and their descendents should not talk about being Americans. They should work and save their money and invest their money and be the equal of Protestant Anglo-Saxon Americans by demonstrating not dependence but initiative. Anglo-Saxon Americans knew how to keep the new immigrants and their children in their place by continually hounding them to rise from it. Almost all American Protestants in the north were morally and politically attached to the Republican party.

One group of immigrants however believed that the niggardly attitude of Republicans to American governments was but one means of disguising in front of the general public the easy ascendancy behind the scenes of Anglo-Saxons to high well-rewarded positions in government, the professions and industry. The Irish-Catholic immigrants were hated by the lower uneducated and bigoted elements of Protestant society along with other European immigrants but the Irish came into America already speaking English and they easily and quickly learned what avenues in governments were open to immigrants that the bigots were helping to keep closed. The Irish at home in Ireland had been for centuries colonized by the English and deprived of access to self-government. In America they promised their fellow European immigrants that once elected mayors of big American cities they would use governments to directly benefit citizens with public works and jobs. The Irish were happy to sin against the niggardly moral and political standards of Republicans by helping create liberal governments. The immigrants from all the nationalities went along with them. The Irish became mayors of large American cities and doled out jobs and political offices to their supporters. Some of them became governors of states. Al Smith in New York, a Catholic, came from this tradition and when he became the democratic governor of New York, he introduced liberal laws and public benefits to citizens of New York state. In 1928 he ran unsuccessfully for president of the United States against Herbert Hoover, but in 1932 Franklin Roosevelt, an aristocrat running as a Democrat, ran voicing the liberal opinions of the Irish and other immigrants and was elected president. Liberalism reached Washington even though Protestant Republicans were against it. But by 1932 the New York stock market had crashed three years before and the economic boom of the roaring 1920s was over. Some form of liberalism was suddenly a necessity even in Washington.

After Wilson, a Democrat, and before Roosevelt, a Democrat, three Republican presidents were elected, Warren Harding, Calvin Coolidge, and Herbert Hoover.

Coolidge was famous for his slogan, "The business of America is business." All the federal commissions that had been created to control the economy and assure wartime production were eliminated. The Federal Government promoted business and was indifferent to its citizens except when they threatened trouble for the sacrosanct middle-class free-enterprise system. In 1920, Chief Justice Mitchell Palmer, with the approval of the president, in one night carried out 33 raids against revolutionaries and arrested 4000 so-called communists. The government promoted and protected businesses. Individuals generally promoted and protected themselves by remaining silent, by working hard, and by acting as "good Americans". Race riots broke out as African-Americans moved north to work in booming industries. The Ku Klux Klan, racist gangs waving the Confederate flag that worthy southerners had fought and died for nobly, hunted down blacks, Jews, Catholics. But business went on booming. Another slogan of the 1920s was "America first". From 1920 to 1930, exports of American products greatly exceeded imports and were mainly sent to a Europe weakened by the war. The Federal Government, aided by decisions of the Supreme Court, succeeded so well in aiding businesses increase profits by merging that by 1930, 50 percent of the industries of the country were concentrated in 200 companies. But why should Americans worry? Why even think about politics? Between 1921 and 1929 industrial production doubled. The gross national product went from 59 billion to 88 billion. The median national income rose from $522 to $716. By 1929, the automobile industry had created more than 26 million cars or one car for every five Americans. In truth, most Americans of the period were indifferent to government and business machinations. They were nationalistic and believed in "America first" but it was difficult to feel deeply joined in sentiment to a nation with a government in Washington so distant and so detached. Americans experienced a kind of quiet awe in respect to Washington. It was a power above and beyond them that select men used in grand classically modeled buildings with majestic columns. Americans passed by daily in their cities and towns bank buildings that were classically modeled too and they inspired awe too as though banks were temples. The business of America was business and the businessmen and politicians were mainly Protestants. Some of them acted aloofly and grandly in a style that fit the grand aloof style of their classical buildings. What America was truly was not a question many people asked as circumstances forced most to be concerned only about their own business.

Herbert Hoover was president in 1929 when the stock market crashed. He was a with-it, get-things-done organizer who had had success internationally running programs to relieve hunger in Belgium and Russia. He believed the government and the economy could be made more efficient by the actions of experts identifying problems and solving them by interfering intelligently. When the crash struck in 1929, he tried to fight in with the force of intelligent government actions and public works projects like the Hoover Dam. He increased corporate taxes and increased income taxes in the top bracket from 25% to 63%. He did more to use the power of the Federal Government positively and universally than his republican predecessors. He formed the top-down government agencies in Washington that Roosevelt, elected president in 1932, would increase to carry out his New Deal federal programs. But Hoover believed strongly in the power of individual acts and volunteerism to aid the economy and that direct government aid to fight unemployment and poverty was wrong. Presidents Harding, Coolidge and Hoover had the same basic message for Americans: do it yourself. In the schools students were taught that they were Americans and their history books related the great patriotic actions of Americans going all the way back to the landing in 1620 in Plymouth Massachusetts of English colonists, the first of many Americans of European origin. It was implicit in everything taught in the schools that Americans like every other people had a nation and that the nation had a national government in Washington. When Republican presidents were in the White House, they echoed the patriotic teaching in the schools but they added to the teaching by their general inaction the lesson that the government of the nation had little or nothing to do either with Americans or for Americans.

When Franklin Roosevelt was elected president in 1932, he tried to make the government in Washington D.C. finally do something for its people directly and concretely. The value of the stock market had fallen 83%. Industrial production was down 40%. Salaries were 60% lower and dividends on stocks 57% lower. 13 million unemployed men were wandering the streets or standing in soup lines. "Only a crazy optimist can deny the dark realities of the moment," said Roosevelt when he took office on March 4 1933. "This country demands that we act and that we act right away." The nation not only existed but it was going to act and act right away. No one saw the irony that while the state governments of 48 states were always acting for their citizens, that while the union of states always remained firm and perpetual, only a war or an economic disaster could cause the national government to act as the vital head of the nation. The Roosevelt New Deal administration created welfare programs like Social Security and created the federal bureaucracies in much like the form they have today, but even with strong government interference and public works and public job programs, the economy never rid itself of huge unemployment until the arrival of the Second World War in 1941. At the time of Roosevelt's second election as president in 1936, 9 million men were unemployed.

Roosevelt, the candidate of the Democratic party, received over 27 million votes in 1936 against 16 million votes for Landon, the Republican. Roosevelt showed Americans for the first time that they had a national government that could and would create programs for them. When the Japanese bombed the American naval base at Pearl Harbor in Hawaii on December 7 1941, Roosevelt aroused the nation in his speeches to military action and Americans followed him united for the first time with a powerful nationalistic fervor. The schools had taught us by their simplistic teachings how to be Americans and we finally at last also felt like Americans. In the schools we were taught nothing about the founding of America as a union of sovereign states. We heard sometimes talk of "states rights" but it was an idea foreign to our spirits and it was associated in our minds closely with the slavery that Abraham Lincoln had abolished and with the backward and repressive treatment of African-Americans in southern states that had followed the Civil War and was still going on. Since we did not care much that we lived in a union of 48 states, all of which were functioning democracies that governed at least 90 percent of all public business, the idea that our United States of America could somehow transform itself to a United States of the World was non-existent. The nationalistic fervor continued, increased by the war effort, and it formed the basis of the national feeling that developed and that continues today. Ironically, Americans experienced for the first time their national government working with them and for them at the moment in history when their government began in earnest working globally for worldwide goals. Americans did not think about globalization even though the Second World War forced them to fight globally. Government leaders in Washington during the war had to think globally. After the war, some leaders even believed that the United States could again become isolationist. Those leaders who continued the global influence of America worldwide had no inkling that they might be working indirectly towards the creation of a United States of the World even though history forced them to work tirelessly throughout the rest of the century to use American military and diplomatic power to unite the states of the world.

10

In 1941 three empires and two large unions of states had formed military alliances and were at war one group against the other globally. Whatever group won would define using its postwar power the political and economic shape of the world of the future. Of the three empires, the British was the largest ruling about 458 million people, one fifth of the world's population, in colonies, dependencies and territories spread out over one quarter of the globe. The Japanese Empire controlled almost 3 million square miles in the Pacific-Asia region making it one of the largest maritime empires in history. It had annexed Korea, occupied Manchuria and parts of Russia and China and threatened the British Empire as far south as Singapore and Burma and even Australia. The third Empire was the European Empire that Germany under Hitler had established by invading and controlling and uniting with its military power several European states. We can think of Italy as a member of the German Empire although it joined Germany as an equal and it was a main power of the Axis alliance of the Japanese Empire with the German/Italian Empire. The United States allied itself with the British Empire against the Axis alliance even before Japan attacked it on December 7 1941 and Germany declared war on it the same month on December 12. Germany had invaded the Soviet Union on June 22 1941 and Russia fought against the German/Italian and Japanese Empires as a third ally joined to the British/American alliance.

Of the five major players in the drama, two, The Soviet Union and the American union were not empires but unions of sovereign states. The Soviet Union, a union of sovereign republics, included the huge territory we normally think of as Russia as one of the republics of the union with a total of 15. The remaining 14 were Armenia, Ukraine, Belarus, Azerbaijan, Uzbekistan, Georgia, Estonia, Kazakhstan, Latvia, Lithuania, Moldova, Turkmenistan, Tajikistan, and Kyrgyzstan. It was a union designed to defend member states from imperialist capitalistic encirclement and defend economic gains that working people had made by taking communistic control of their economies. The declaration of 1922 forming the union said that it was a voluntary union of peoples with equal rights and each Soviet republic retained the right to freely secede from the union. It is debatable how much political freedom each republic had and under the dictatorship of Joseph Stalin from Moscow they had little if any but in June of 1941 when an army of 4 million Europeans led by Germany attacked the union, freedom no longer mattered. Only an all-out patriotic war to save Russia mattered.

The Russian revolutionaries in setting up the Soviet Union were at least thinking of the shape of the new world of the future in terms of a union of states. They were opposed to the European and Japanese empires that ruled the world widely except in parts of South America and in North America south of Canada, a self-ruling British colony. Britain and America began their alliance even before America entered the war at the Conference of Placentia in Newfoundland in August 1941. President Roosevelt and Winston Churchill, the British head of state, met and agreed to the Atlantic Charter. Churchill understood the goal of the charter to be the defeat of Fascism and the restoration of the sovereignty of occupied states. Franklin Roosevelt understood the goal differently. He understood the alliance as a chance to put an end to imperialism. Roosevelt told Churchill, "I can't believe that we can fight a war against fascist slavery, and at the same time not work to free people all over the world from a backward colonial policy. The peace cannot include any continued despotism ... Equality of peoples involves the utmost freedom of competitive trade." Roosevelt early in the alliance was thus restating Wilsonian principles of free peoples and free trade worldwide. The British needed the alliance with America desperately. Roosevelt was trying to trade America's help for the end of imperialism. He wanted to include in the charter the words, ".. without discrimination to further the enjoyment by all states, great or small, victor or vanquished, of access, on equal terms, to the trade and to the raw materials of the world ...". Churchill insisted that rather than the words, "without discrimination", the charter should read instead, "with due respect to their existing obligations". The debate and conflict in the alliance between British imperialism and the American vision of free independent states worldwide continued. After the Lend-Lease Agreement was signed five months later supplying Britain with products from the huge American economy, Roosevelt is supposed to have told his son Elliot, "I've tried to make it clear to Winston - and the others - that, while we're their allies and in it to victory by their side, they must never get the idea that we're in it just to help them hang on to the archaic, medieval Empire ideas ... Great Britain signed [sic] the Atlantic Charter. I hope they realize the United States Government means to make them live up to it." The Soviet union of states and the American union of states were happy to be allied with the British Empire in the worldwide war to destroy Fascism but they were both also the enemies of British imperialism.

By November of 1941 the German-led armies in Russia had reached the outskirts of Leningrad and Moscow. It was clear to everyone that the Soviet Union was on its way down and out and that after Hitler's armies took Moscow, nothing could stop them reaching all across Siberia to the Pacific Ocean to link up with territories of the Japanese Empire. Hitler would soon have the largest empire in the world extending from France on the west to the Pacific coast of Russia in the east. In this dire circumstance, the British Empire and America joined both politically and militarily. They created *de facto* a new world union of Britain and British colonies and possessions and 48 American states and possessions. They had to assume Russia would soon be defeated and that Hitler with a victorious army of more than 4 million men possessing all the resources of Europe and the Soviet Union could never be opposed successfully by them in a land war in Europe. They immediately decided to oppose Hitler in the air and on the seas. Industrial production in the

United States increased 150 percent by 1943. On December 7 when the Japanese bombed Pearl Harbor, America had 1,157 combat airplanes. In 5 years, it constructed 297,000. It had about 1000 tanks and in 5 years had 86,338. Year by year it was able to double and triple the tonnage of its shipbuilding. The British and Americans were preparing to defend the British Empire and the union of American states worldwide by air and by sea. When Hitler completed the conquest of Russia, they would be able to negotiate peace with him from a position of strength or else fight him outside of Europe and Russia with strength. It is probable that the Japanese bombed Pearl Harbor in Hawaii because they were confidant that the Soviet Union would be soon out of the war and they wished to be in a position to claim the Hawaiian Islands at a future peace conference. Three empires and the American union of states were ready to divide up the world as soon as the Soviet Union went down. But the Soviet Union did not go down and allied with the American union and the British Empire, it helped destroy the German and Japanese empires and the two victorious unions of states were the powers after the war who shaped the world of the future as it got rid of all empires worldwide and saw the rise globally of new independent states.

The British provided the logic that gave a positive slant to the end of their empire and the end of the other European empires. It was a costly business keeping colonies. The ruling European country had to build infrastructures in its colonies, roads, railroads, courts, schools etc. and provide police and military protection in order to steal the colony's raw materials. Now, the logic went, each colony could become a nation with borders well defined on maps and as each emerged as a self-governing body paying with its currency for necessary infrastructures, rich developed nations could simply enter the new nations and buy their raw materials at bargain prices since the exchange rate between a rich country and a poor country would be highly favorable to the rich country. And any plant set up in a new nation by a foreign corporation to process locally raw materials could hire locals at dirt cheap wages and be certain that the former European state or America would enter with military force if the free enterprise of foreign corporations were threatened by communist revolutionaries. The new states could not possibly have the capacity to produce the finished products available in the rich states and these could be exported and sold in the new nations to the few who could afford them. Surely there was a cynical side to the logic but on the other hand it was a realistic logic that simply outlined in economic terms the fate of the new developing nations. In the postwar years of the 1950s and 1960s, many new states were appearing worldwide and soon the whole globe was covered with states with clearly defined borders. The existence of states worldwide meant they could be united worldwide. The British and Americans formed the United Nations at the beginning of their wartime alliance. It was established after the war in New York City. The UN was a worldwide union of sovereign states. No thought at all was yet given to the idea of a worldwide union of sovereign states who would each accept limited sovereignty and grant limited sovereignty to a central government to which they would send representatives to make universal laws for their world union.

One of the principles of such a union would be that any citizen of any state in the union would have the absolute right to move to and live and work in any state in the union and have full rights as a citizen in a new state simply by establishing residence in it. This principle was already established by law in the union of 48 states in America but the idea of limiting sovereignty in states worldwide was never suggested to them for the reason that it was a totally hostile idea. Every people wanted their state free and democratic and only full sovereignty seemed to them to guarantee freedom and democracy. America certainly was far from proposing to the new states in the postwar years that they apply to the American Congress and become new states of the American union. But America nonetheless began pursuing goals of freedom and democracy for states throughout the world that put in place piece by piece some principles that foreshadowed some of the principles of a future union worldwide of states with limited sovereignty. Another principle of such a union would be the absolute right and obligation of each member state to get rid altogether of a large national military force and at the same time be absolutely secure from invasion by a hostile state because each state would be protected by a large professional army maintained by the central government of the union.

In 1950 the state of South Korea was invaded by forces from North Korea. America immediately established under President Truman that it would not allow any state outside the control of the Soviet Union to be invaded. Truman sent the American army to Korea and aided by troops from several countries worldwide it drove the invaders out of South Korea. The principle that a state might become free from the worry of invasion and function as a democracy if it formed some kind of union with a powerful foreign government was established. A third principle of the United States of the World, a worldwide union that still no one envisioned, is that a member state freed from the expense of maintaining an army and freed from all restraints on its trade with member states worldwide, would prosper. South Korea prospered. It lost very little of its national independence by alliance with America and it prospered. It prospered mightily. It foreshadowed a condition that all states might one day enjoy if only world conditions might in the future reveal to them that full sovereignty is not the key to real democracy and prosperity and that a just limitation of their sovereignty in a world union of democratic states each forced by law to remain democratic is the key.

The full sovereignty of the new developing states included the right to create their own army to defend themselves and it meant they were free to create and build up their state's economy in any way they wished. Only the future would tell how well they progressed under these conditions. Meanwhile three states, Japan, Germany and Italy were forced as losers in the war to live without the expense of funding military forces and to function free of the fear of invasion protected by the American military. The US after the war no longer respected the borders of nation-states and in the Cold War it was waging against the Soviet Union it considered itself free to interfere economically, militarily and politically inside states wherever necessary to form or support free-enterprise economies. It established military bases in Japan, Germany and Italy and interfered politically when necessary to keep their economies on the right capitalistic path. In Italy it worked internally by various means to defeat the elections of communists who nearly took over the national government. The three defeated nations thus enjoyed before any other states in the world by union with a powerful external government four principles of a future United States of the World: the right and obligation not to build up and maintain a large military, the right and obligation to maintain a democratic government or be forced to create one by the power of an external government, the right to be free of invasion by a foreign state, and the right to the economic prosperity that would be the result. Japan, Germany and Italy prospered mightily, astoundingly. The only right of future members of the United States of the World that the three did not enjoy was the right of their citizens to live and work and be citizens of any state in a union worldwide with the enjoyment of full political rights simply by establishing residency in the state of their choice. However, the three states did enjoy the right to sell the products of their free enterprise free of tariffs in the 48 states in America and their corporations were free to establish themselves in America or anywhere worldwide along side of American corporations who like their government no longer respected the borders of states. For the US government and American corporations any state was ripe to be penetrated for the establishment of American values and for profit.

The Soviet Union increased its political power by alliances or control over Bulgaria, Cuba, Czechoslovakia, East Germany, Hungary, Poland and Romania. China, Yugoslavia and Albania were also communistic but free of control by Moscow. The Cold War was a struggle between the values and economic practices of the middle class and the working class. America and Russia penetrated states worldwide and tried to set up either a capitalistic or communistic system. The difference was that middle-class economies had been thriving and developing in Europe for nearly a thousand years and in America middle-class practices and values were so widespread that there was simply one class, from the extremely rich to the extremely poor, with people with middle-class values located everywhere and not just in the middle. The free European states and the American states had a proven economic system that worked because it was based on initiative and greed. The Russian system was actually less revolutionary than the American system. The Russian system eliminated the drive for profits and the American system let it loose. It was virtually decided already at the beginning of the Cold War which system was more profitable and which would create after years of struggle the world of the future. In Europe the middle class had isolated itself from the other classes and struggled to gain power over them. It developed new revolutionary values based on science, rationalism and materialism. It considered itself unique and believed at the same time that its values were universal. The middle class in Europe in its pride was sure that members of other classes envied it and secretly wished to adopt its values. American economic and educational practices eliminated the exclusiveness and pettiness of middle-class bigwigs and made middle-class values revolutionary by universalizing them as a new way of life for all humanity. The worker's paradise that bureaucrats in Moscow were creating by five-year plans that plodded along five years at a time to new five-year plans never materialized on earth and the paradise that already existed at the top of the bureaucratic ladder was common to few. The American Federal Government had no desire to govern directly its own people or any right to govern foreign peoples. Its business was to interfere in its own states to assure democratic laws and free enterprise and to penetrate foreign states to upset customary economic and political practices and force states by injecting American corporations or American business practices into their economies to rebel against their outdated policies and practices.

In the Second World War, Moscow had led the Soviet Union's armies to Berlin and victory at a cost of 20 million dead. Now it had to wage another war worldwide to defend a new working-class economic system and working-class values. It was an all out war, truly worldwide, that echoed in its fashion the hundred years life-or-death struggle between Rome and Carthage that decided who would rule the huge empire that surrounded in the ancient world the Mediterranean Sea. During the three Punic wars between Rome and Carthage, and the Cold war between Washington and Moscow there was no free thought. You were either for what Rome represented or what Carthage represented, for what Washington represented or what Moscow represented. The middle class, the bourgeoisie, had already done all the thinking for hundreds of years and no more was necessary. In fact, any new unusual thought during the postwar period was a kind of treason against established thought and established political and economic systems that the best people in both unions of states were fighting for worldwide. Thought in the second half of the twentieth century in the free world lost its individual human dimension and this was clearly reflected in the abstract art of the period. Soviet working-class art pictured working men and women with faces so monumentally enthused for the heroic tasks they were accomplishing that it was nearly grotesque. Free thought was out. The philosopher Hegel had demonstrated over a hundred years previously that there was no free thought anyway. Thought seemed free for a while and even inspirational but it did not last. One thought was quickly overcome by some contrary thought. Hegel showed clearly in his *Philosophy of History* that all so called free thought was just some partial manifestation at some stage or another in world history of the universal spirit evolving and advancing through stages. The goal of history according to Hegel was not freedom to think freely but freedom itself. And this freedom could only be realized in a state controlled by bourgeois politicians with bourgeois values. "The essential being," Hegel wrote, "is the union of the subjective with the rational will: it is the moral whole, the state, which is that form of reality in which the individual has and enjoys his freedom". In America in the 1940s and 1950s we enjoyed this kind of freedom as long as we took loyalty oaths and said nothing and did nothing to oppose the goons enjoying the freedom of accusing loyal Americans of being communists. The American union and the Soviet Union made both free thought and conventional weapons obsolete. They were threatening each other not only with opposing ideologies but with atom and hydrogen bombs. They both had plenty of these bombs in projectiles ready to fly.

The National Security Act of 1947 passed by the American Congress set up the National Security Council to advise the American president on matters of national security. The council's members included the Central Intelligence Agency, in charge of worldwide espionage, and the Joint Chiefs of Staff, in charge of worldwide war. In effect, Congress set up a secret branch of the Federal Government to carry out policies conceived in secret behind the scenes. Abraham Lincoln had conceived his policy for war in secret behind the scenes. The Congress in 1947 felt America's freedom and economic way of life so threatened by

Moscow that it bestowed on the president openly the dictatorial powers that Lincoln had had to usurp. Moscow took similar extreme steps to protect its centralized power and concoct plots to overthrow capitalist systems in states worldwide. Free nations took similar steps. Britain was so strongly allied with America against Moscow that it merged its national intelligence agency with the American Central Intelligence Agency, the CIA. Nations everywhere had to take extreme steps. They had to line up behind the new Rome or the new Carthage, behind Washington or Moscow.

Both powers in the Cold War controlled a union of states and were trying to create a union of the rest of the states in the world by penetrating them where possible and remodeling their political and economic system using their own system as a model. Strangely, as the Cold War progressed it became clear to keen observers that the competition between Washington and Moscow helped reinforce their power at home and produced in developed and developing states a clear either-or choice politically and economically that brought about a kind of stability because of the conflict. Washington penetrated states in one of three ways and often in a combination of the three. First, it offered states direct monetary aid or aided them by establishing military bases and by training their armed forces. Secondly, it penetrated them by aiding its corporations establish themselves in states to extract their natural resources. This was an altered form of the old imperialism whose goal was to mine raw minerals and ship them home to the mother country where they were scarce. The third way was to penetrate richer and more advanced countries worldwide by helping export big American corporations to establish themselves in foreign nations and compete directly with native business organizations. None of the three produced economic conditions in the developing nations that directly set in motion a system to fight the general poverty in place among the majority of a population. Frustration and anger developed as states grew richer from foreign intervention and investment but little of the riches reached the mass of the population Here was where Moscow fit in nicely. It alone offered an economic system that seemed designed to directly eliminate poverty. Moscow entered a developing country and aided revolutionaries militarily who had no choice but to be communists for immediate aid and to nourish their hope to establish a future economy that might work for all. Moscow's military penetration or possible penetration in turn justified Washington's military and espionage actions in states to prevent or overthrow communist governments. It was a *quid pro quo*. My penetration is justified because of your penetration and you are free to penetrate where I have already penetrated. Culturally and historically speaking, in the old middle-class- run nation-states of Europe, the bourgeoisie developed their riches on the backs of workers' labor with wages lower than necessary. They did nothing at all to produce riches universally for all classes. In the Cold War, the same conflict played itself out on a global and international stage. Washington played the bourgeois, Moscow the worker. Middle-class businessmen went all over the world aided by American diplomacy and its military enriching only themselves and corrupt officials. People in states worldwide with no part in the play suffered. Moscow did its best to help them and give them hope but it had a losing role in the play because the part it played led nowhere.

The world outside the United States after the Second World War was too poor to buy the products American industry could produce. Instead of exporting its production, America decided to export instead its means of production. By the end of the 1950s, American corporations had invested 30 billion dollars to establish themselves worldwide and of the 6000 enterprises established a half of them, 3000 businesses, were in Europe. A few advanced European thinkers in the 1960s realized with amazement that American corporations were doing much more in Europe to unite European states into united economies than their Common Market. The American corporations cared little about national borders and they had invented creative ways of organizing and reorganizing the way they did business that made traditional European ways of doing business seem sterile. Stimulated by technical research funded by the Federal Government to compete with new Soviet technical advances, constant technical innovation had become the ruling activity of American corporations. In America, government administrators, industrial managers, university economists, engineers and scientists were creating new rational strategies to integrate factors of

production that were constantly innovating the structures of corporations. The American corporations used the same strategies in Europe.
American corporations were taking over European industries so rapidly
that many Europeans feared that they would soon be producing as much
in Europe as European corporations. The governments of European
nation-states found themselves facing a difficult dilemma: if they
allowed the American corporations to install themselves in their nation,
they risked condemning their native industry to a secondary role, but if
they restricted American corporations, they would move to a neighboring nation and deprive an unreceptive nation of development that it
needed. Although Europeans believed American corporations invested
overseas for the national benefit of the American nation, American
corporations in Europe employed Europeans and very few Americans
and paid them salaries significantly higher than European corporations. The American corporations installed in Europe directly reduced
possible exports from the United States because those using advanced
techniques produced advanced products so necessary for European
consumption that Europeans would have had to import them from the
US if American corporations were not manufacturing them in Europe.
A saving grace to the situation was of course that Europeans could invest
in the American corporations and earn money from the economic progress as stockholders. Ironically American corporations financed their
European enterprises with 90% of the funds coming from European
investors and just 10% from Americans. What Europeans were witnessing
was the first explosions of the war to create multinational corporations
worldwide. In the battles of the 1960s, computers and advanced communications were being introduced as new weapons whose importance was
destined to grow and aid exponentially the installation of multinational
corporations worldwide. European corporations soon adopted the new
American business methods and the new technologies and learned to
move some of their corporations into global positions. Eventually, by
the 1970s and 1980s, underdeveloped countries like China and India
were able to use for free production techniques that were started and
developed in America and take gigantic developmental steps quickly.
Most of the smaller developing countries never realized enough capital

from their small savings to invest profitably in local industry. Their rich citizens were forced by circumstances to invest their savings in multinational corporations and earn profits from industries outside their native states. Multinational corporations were alive and well globally hoping from state to state wherever the lure of profits enticed them and while the world accepted multinational corporations, no one had any thought yet of multistate citizenship. Individuals did not yet have the right to hop from nation to nation for their betterment.

The United States of America and the united states of the Soviet Union provided firm political bases at home for Washington and Moscow to operate worldwide but the base in each weakened in the 1950s and in the 1960s began to crack. In the US the people were united politically by the fear of communists somehow taking over and destroying their way of life. In the USSR the people were united by the fear of the dictator Joseph Stalin. Stalin died in 1956 and when his successor Nikita Khrushchev denounced him and his type of rule and called for liberalization, Hungarians revolted and were put down by Russian tanks but they showed that the foundation of the communist system was weak and could be shaken. In 1968 the Czechoslovakians succeeded for a while in liberalizing economic practices and were repressed by Moscow but they made the need to liberalize a continuing idea in peoples' minds. Already in 1963 during the Cuban Missile Crisis, Washington and Moscow had threatened one another with nuclear war and their leaders, Khrushchev and Kennedy, had bravely withstood their hawkish military establishments who wanted to pull the triggers. Washington and Moscow showed when real war was possible that neither of them wanted it. The compromise and the peace that resulted revealed that the Cold War was not as serious a war as it had seemed although the military hawks gained again the upper hand when events forced both Khrushchev and Kennedy from power. President Lyndon Johnson, who succeeded Kennedy, went full speed ahead with the war in Vietnam and when Richard Nixon was elected president in 1968, he continued the war even though in his election campaign he had suggested that he would end it. Nixon's political career had been nourished by anticommunism. He got himself elected to Congress from California in 1946 by denouncing communism and arousing fear among his voters of traitorous American communists in their midst. There were few communists in California in 1946 but in 1968 President Nixon had real communist enemies in Vietnam in his gun's sight and he pulled the trigger and kept pulling it. Even while American troops were leaving Vietnam, he continued bombing communists with massive air attacks. Then the last thing in the world that an habitual cold warrior like Nixon might imagine happening happened: half of the American people denounced the war in Vietnam and very directly announced to Washington in massive public demonstrations that they were sick to death of being forced to hate communism and show their loyalty to Washington by supporting wars against communists. They were telling Nixon and the world that they were totally sick of the Cold War. The war in Vietnam seemed to people who were thoroughly engrained with middle-class American values unnecessary and unjustified. They wanted a different world. Wars and ideological conflicts between states seemed out of date and on their way out. Forces independent of any particular part of the world were busy changing the world and people worldwide sensed the changes going on and wanted to be a part of them. The nation-state of the past was on the way out too but one leader, Charles de Gaulle, had tried to inspire France to become a nationalistic bulwark against the new forms of political and economic life that were emerging worldwide and transcending national boundaries. The French rebelled in May and June of 1968 with fierce anti-government protests against something they could not define to themselves except very vaguely but they tore up streets in Paris anyway and fought police behind barricades for changes they sensed already on the way in the world and that they wanted for themselves locally. De Gaulle was forced out of office by the new world in formation that suddenly blew up in his face. Meanwhile Richard Nixon kept up his massive bombing of Cambodia and Vietnam and was not forced out of power until 1974. Nixon the cold warrior and the devoted anticommunist had visited Moscow in 1972 and 1974 and tried to get the communist leaders in the Kremlin to influence their allies, the communist leaders in Vietnam, to accept peace with America on Nixon's terms. Capitalists and communists were playing antagonistic roles on stages around the globe but behind the scenes they hobnobbed together and respected the conflicting parts each played. Nixon signed trade and arms control agreements with Moscow and gained their help in influencing Vietnamese leaders to end the war. Nixon visited Chinese communists in 1972 to see what role they might be willing to play in the global theater. Nixon's visit to China did begin the destruction of the Chinese communist system but by the 1970s new advanced technologies for organizing the factors of production were available universally and the Chinese communists could not resist applying them to their economy which was rich already with massive supplies of local cheap human labor. Nixon merely opened the door. Multinational corporations were showing the roads to follow that lead to the new world and the Chinese rushed out through Nixon's open door and flew down all the roads. Nixon resigned as president in 1974 forced out of office by disgraceful undemocratic operations that he had conducted behind the scenes to steal information that might have helped him suppress American freedoms. On his last day in Washington, Americans watched on television as he waved goodbye and got on an airplane. He was waving goodbye too to the Cold War.

11

But the Cold War went on for another seventeen years. The global actions of Washington went on as usual. The president who succeeded Nixon, Gerald Ford, almost immediately after taking power ordered an invasion of a Cambodian island without consulting Congress. In 1976 only 53% of Americans voted. Carter, a Democrat, was elected campaigning and winning the presidency by making unfulfilled promises to a disillusioned people. The public medias grew in power and influence but they gave no direct voice to thousands of local groups campaigning for environmental protection, women's rights, or against homelessness and military spending. American corporations in Europe, Latin America, Asia and Africa continued making billions of dollars in profits. "The world and its treasures", to use Leo Tolstoy's phrase, "is booty for the bold." American corporations supported by American diplomacy and its military were the boldest of the bold. They got at least 90% of their diamonds, platinum, coffee, mercury, rubber, cobalt, manganese, chrome and aluminum from foreign states. Ronald Reagan elected president in 1980 cut federal benefits to the poor, lowered income taxes for the wealthy, increased the military budget, filled the federal court system with conservative judges, and destroyed revolutionary movements in the Caribbean and elsewhere. Reagan had to wait two years in office to invade a state but he did so in 1982 when he sent troops into Lebanon. In a survey conducted by the *New York Times* in 1976, over half of the respondents said that public officials didn't care about them. They should have answered instead that the public officials in their state governments had no choice but to care about them and that the officials in the Federal Government who received trillions of dollars in income taxes were authorized by their Constitution to care about Americans very little or not at all. Washington's interests world-wide were so extensive and so demanding of its attention because of the Cold War that the Federal Government seemed to dominate American life even more indirectly than as usual and in a way that seemed to many Americans to be equivalent to indifference. It may be that officials in Moscow ruling Russia, a nation-state, never realized that Washington was not the central government of a nation-state and that this was the source of its overwhelming power to wage the Cold War endlessly. When Michael Gorbachev proposed to begin a process to end the Cold War in 1986 in a conference with Ronald Reagan in Reykjavik Iceland, Reagan refused his offer. When George Bush was elected president in 1988, Gorbachev visited him in Washington in 1989 already having taken liberal steps within the Soviet Union to end the Cold War but Bush was not eager to end the Cold War so quickly. He wanted to go slowly. It was cash on the barrelhead the Cold War. It was painful for cold warriors to let it go.

Communism as an economic system had not been a viable system for years but when Moscow dissolved the USSR in 1991 it ended not only communism but also a union of states. It meant that the new free states in Eastern Europe and those to the south of Russia as well as China and Russia itself were now open to multinational corporations for investment. Here was an extraordinary new burst of freedom for big corporations originating anywhere in any nation to make a lot of money. All they needed to satisfy their greed was a huge military power positioned with its ships and its aircraft and its military all over the globe to make their investments secure. Washington possessing a government well funded and freed by its Constitution from governing its people by direct actions in their states was ready and eager to secure the world now free of communist nations for multinational corporations. America had no respect for the borders of nation-states during the Cold War and in her new role as the military champion of multinational corporations she made it clear that no state anywhere had the right to invade any state and that she would defend any and all states from invasion. The dictator of Iraq, Saddam Hussein, had been tolerated by Washington but he invaded Kuwait in 1991 violating the new rules of the international game. President George Bush went to war at once and drove Hussein's forces back into Iraq dropping tons of bombs on his territory on a scale comparable to Richard Nixon's bombardment of Cambodia. Other nations joined Bush's war against Iraq showing by their actions that they agreed with the new worldwide rule that all states were now free from the threat of invasion. Old-style nation-state wars did break out in the 1990s in the Balkans but the states involved were forced to retreat behind their borders by international intervention and by an American bombardment under President Clinton. In the Near East, Israel and neighboring states still lived with the threat of invasion but this was a local matter. Universally no state was threatened by invasion and America had military bases in 177 nations and its navy around the world and over 2 million people in its military to back up the new worldwide deal. However leaders of sovereign states were still free to use their local military forces against their own people. Prevention of civil wars was not a part of the deal. As long as heads of states did nothing with their military against multinational corporations, they had a free hand to do what they wished internally and rule their own people by force. They received monies from corporations established on their national land either legitimately or corruptly and had no reason to interfere with their work.

The rich located anywhere in the world profited from investments in corporations established throughout the world. The new burst of profits gained worldwide by corporations did not reach down into the hands of the majority of people worldwide except sometimes in trickles. Voices were raised everywhere criticizing corporations but they had little effect because their criticism was wrong. Wealth no longer existed in the world as in the past in the form of raw materials or as a result of applying the technologies of the past to industrial production. A large part of the wealth now produced was the result not only of advanced technologies but also from advancements in computers and communications that allowed creative forms of business structures unknown previously. Political freedom, real political freedom, also was an essential factor in producing wealth because such freedom went hand in hand with revolutionary new types of banking practices that created money for big and small business enterprises wherever opportunities presented themselves. Political freedom in turn can exist stably only when it is supported and protected by advanced judicial and educational systems both of which are necessary to help protect individual citizens from corrupt officials and the excesses of corporations. Wealth could now be created universally in states who were developed enough to adapt the new practices used by big multinational corporations to work for the goals locally of their citizens. Corporations were greedy but not necessarily bad. Big corporations were often the best means available to produce wealth and sometimes the only means.

Corporations are here to stay and it is false and useless to criticize them as the source of the world's evils. It is the inhuman *indifference* of corporations to the people they employ and to the people outside their orbit that helps create the shamefully superficial forms of individual behavior that are visible everywhere and characterize the beginning years of the twenty-first century. People must prepare themselves mentally to work for corporations to be successful economically and this comes at a great cost to their individuality and to their openness to what is true. Corporations create by their indifference not only products and profits but an ambiance full of people constrained in their self-development to low-end self-development. The United States government in its totality is a super corporation richer with its trillions of dollars of income than any government of the past ever even dreamed possible. It is made up of hundreds of agencies and departments of all sorts, public corporations financed by public taxes, with purposes outlined for them by laws created by the US Congress. They add more indifference to the immense list of private corporations also acting indifferently. But it is false and useless to criticize the Federal Government's body of public corporations as the source of evil. Public corporations have good goals and it is certainly true that some forms of goodness can and must be produced indifferently. It is not wrong for the US government to organize the world so that corporations owned by the rich can be free and secure worldwide to create wealth and enjoy profits. It is wrong however for the US government having the means to grant universal democracy and economic freedom guaranteed by law to all people worldwide to instead strive worldwide only for the freedom of multinational corporations. We Americans fund by our income taxes and other taxes the Federal Government's worldwide power and we have a political and moral right to enjoy the freedoms and the fruits of its power as well as corporations.

What are we Americans going to do? Are we going to forget completely and forever because of the abusive negative acts against American states of Abraham Lincoln that we are a union of 50 independent sovereign states? We possess the most successful and the most radical political system ever created on earth for guaranteeing by law democratic governments for our states and our union of states has been the main source of exceptional economic development for our citizens. Are we going to sit back and do nothing to help the rest of the world enjoy the benefits of the system that we enjoy and that many states in the world now need? Washington gained enormous power for itself internally and externally in the twentieth century but it is false and wrong for us to believe that this power must necessarily be used only to dominate our states and to influence openly and secretly foreign states throughout the world. Washington's worldwide power is precisely a condition necessary to produce freedom and goodness for us and everyone else in the world because only worldwide power can guarantee freedom and universal human rights worldwide. The Washington government is also the only well funded independent powerful organization existing in the world that has the material means and the political power to reduce and eliminate the threats to the world's environment like global warming. What to do? We must be loyal to Washington and support its actions around the world because they are mostly designed for the world's welfare. We must accept in good faith whatever it decides is the supreme law of our perpetual union. But we and everyone else in the world can not hide from the fact that Washington is the new Rome. We are all dependent on it already to greater or lesser degrees for our world's welfare. But our loyalty to Washington should not require us Americans to do nothing. We must act as states. We have rights as states guaranteed by our Constitution. We must make America begin listening to voices that come not only from Washington but also from the heart and soul of what American history has made us, a union of sovereign states. We must bust out of our comfortable bubble and realize that the economy of our union of states can become expansive in a revolutionary and positive way if we lighten the national responsibilities of Washington and give it instead the burden of interstate leadership on a worldwide scale. Our job is to invite all states in the world to join our union of states in order to assure by our laws and our Constitution their existence as democracies and their economic development. If foreign states, rich or poor, were to join our union, two doors to increased prosperity would open immediately. The citizens in a newly admitted state would be guaranteed a democratic government and the right to work and live as a citizen of any one of more than 50 states. At the same time, every business at any level established in any state of the union, small businesses as well as large corporations, would be guaranteed the same economic freedom and the same property rights in new states that are now enjoyed in the present 50 American states. Small banks could move an office to a new state as easily as they now move to the present member states of the union and open for business using a banking system that is the most radical and the most practical ever invented. Small construction companies could move easily without the aid of American diplomats to any new state and use their know-how to create new jobs and expansive new development. Holes would be suddenly punched in our bubble and the fresh air of new possibilities would flow in that could grow wider and wider as more and more states unburden themselves of dead national forms and reform. New states that join our union will send immediately two senators each to join in the deliberations of Washington's senate. Their citizens elected to the House of Representatives will also go to the Congress on Capitol Hill in Washington and pass universal laws designed to establish and guarantee a whole list of unalienable human rights for all people worldwide. The federal judiciary and the

Federal Bureau of Investigation, the FBI, will have access by right to all states and will free all citizens of all member states worldwide from the tyrannical practices of corrupt politicians using state powers for themselves rather than for the just ambitions of their people. Multinational corporations supported by the American military and by American diplomats have failed to develop economies in the states they enter at the middle and lower ends. By adopting for their states advanced banking and management practices modeled after those in the current American states and by instituting advanced educational and judiciary systems modeled also after the practices in American states, new states will assure themselves not only democratic political freedoms but also general economic development for all their citizens. Worldwide multinational corporations must not make the only waves of the future. Worldwide multistate citizenship should make the most powerful wave of all. Such a wave could produce new bursts of freedom for individual citizens and new economic opportunities because of the vastly expanded possibilities for human development that membership in our union will allow.

No officials of the Federal Government except those elected to the Congress of the United States have the right under the Constitution to vote for bills to admit or reject new states. We should never elect in the future any candidate to Congress who is not willing to vote for new states to join and to expand our union. The President has the right to veto such bills but the Congress has the right to override his veto. Neither the Department of State nor the Defense Department nor officials of any other agency or department of the Federal Government have any right at all in the matter. Article IV section 3. of the Constitution states this power clearly, "New States may be admitted by the Congress into this Union." We Americans already live in a union of states that has been expanding by admitting new states since the union was founded with 13 states in 1787. Since then Congress has admitted 37 new states. Organizing sovereign states into a union with a duly constituted central government has been a political work in progress throughout American history. It must continue in order to continue to assure the existence of governments in our states with full democratic rights and to assure as well democratic governments to newly admitted states. Article IV Section 4. of the US Constitution states, "The United States shall guarantee to every State in the Union a Republican Form of Government, and protect each of them from invasion".

We need to give not only the Federal Government in Washington but also the foreign states around the world the means to operate their governments and their economies in a balanced and positive manner that will surely produce more prosperity and more good for foreign peoples and for ourselves than exists now. In 2002 the second Bush elected president, George W. Bush, decided to launch an invasion of the sovereign state of Iraq without any reasonable justification. He caused the death of thousands of innocent people because he not only conquered the country but then failed completely to pacify it by establishing a judicial system backed by an appropriate and effective police force. Clearly this disaster showed once again both that the Federal Government has little interest in being only a national government of the United States and that it is already operating for good or for ill as a de facto international government. The admission of new states to our union will accomplish the stated international goals of Washington of democracy for foreign states and of free economic development for them in the global economy. This should give balance to Washington's international behavior by giving it the means to develop the world politically and economically in a legitimate and concrete form. It should give up vague talk of freedom and democracy for foreign states and invite them all to join its union and actually experience freedom and democracy. Washington can act directly in the interests of Americans by adopting the policy of transforming itself to the central government of a world union of states. The United States of the World with Washington at its center as a duly constituted government will give every American the international opportunities for business and employment that Washington has been providing rich corporations. At the same time it will provide all corporations and all businesses at any level with far lower operating costs. No longer will expensive quid pro quo international bargaining be necessary between diplomats and businessmen and politicians in national states to allow businesses and individuals to cross borders and reconcile their activities with local laws. The US government now has the power, granted it by the Constitution, to rule over interstate commerce and the wealth of the world will increase dramatically as Washington also governs indirectly new states and begins promoting interstate commerce universally.

Many new developing states are disturbed by tribal, ethnic and religious differences that thwart their political and economic development because corrupt politicians exacerbate such differences to gain power. Once admitted to the American union, this will no longer be allowed by Washington. The people of newly admitted states will have double citizenship, citizenship in the state of their choice and citizenship in the United States. The many agencies and departments in Washington established by Congress for good purposes as aids to American state governments will also aid the governments of new states. New states must agree to limit their sovereignty by giving up their right to make war on other states and to conduct diplomatic relations with them and they must obey laws passed by the Congress in Washington but by way of exchange their citizens will vote for representatives not only to the local democratic government of their state but also vote and send representatives to the Congress in Washington. We Americans have learned that the limited sovereignty of our states instead of limiting democracy and freedom produces and secures them and that they are the vital conditions of advanced economic development. We want to increase our opportunities for new economic ventures by locating in newly admitted states in our union and in turn we want foreign states to create new opportunities for their citizens by giving them the right to locate in any state of our union by joining our union. Any new state admitted to the US union must continue as a democratic government or else form such a government. An inviolable democratic government and an absolute freedom from the threat of invasion should be the goal of all the states in the world. It should also be their goal to give their citizens the right to full citizenship in any state of their union of states simply by establishing residence in a state of their choice.

The fundamental idea of any world union of states must be that the central government possess sovereign powers that are strictly limited and defined in a Constitution. The Federal Government of America has exclusive power only over military affairs and diplomacy. It also has power to regulate interstate commerce and to maintain a federal legal system that can overturn state and federal laws and decisions of state courts, but neither of these powers are absolute and they would be necessary in any case to assure the just workings of an international union of states. No government with full national sovereignty can ever transform itself to the central government of a world union. The US government in Washington in the District of Columbia possesses neither full sovereignty nor any national territory over which it rules as a sovereign power. It acts as the national government of a nation-state only when relating to nation-states throughout the world in matters of war and diplomacy. Within the American union of states, it acts as the hub of a large wheel of 50 states who govern themselves and also send representatives to the center of the wheel in Washington DC to make laws necessary to keep the wheel spinning justly.

No political entity called "America" exists. The United States of America are not all on the continent of North America. The state of Hawaii, admitted to the union in 1959, is composed of a group of islands near the middle of the Pacific Ocean. The correct name of the present union should be, "The United States of North America and the Pacific". We do call one another "Americans" even though we were not born in "America" but in one of 50 states. The Federal Government located in the District of Columbia has always governed the several states very little or not at all. An American becomes a citizen of the state where he is born and automatically also a citizen of the US. However he is born in a state, educated by a state, hospitalized in a state certified hospital, transported on state roads and transportation systems, married by a state, judged mostly in state courts, guarded by state police, protected by state firemen and dies in a state with his money deposited in a state bank. What does the Federal Government do during his life that directly affects him? It gives him the means to fight in war, assures his right to interstate commerce and to citizenship in any state he may choose to live in, and tells him when the laws of his state violate the Constitution. It also absolves the state where he resides of the necessity to establish diplomatic relations with other states in the world. The most important thing the Federal Government does for states is obey the Constitution by guaranteeing a democratic government to each state. It conducts its pro democratic operations admirably. The United States Department of Justice and the FBI, the Federal Bureau of Investigation, regularly put corrupt state politicians, most of them democratically elected, in jail. The big cat from Washington is ever eager to pounce on and punish mice in state governments stealing the people's cheese.

On September 9 2011, Salvatore F. DiMasi, a former Speaker of the House of Representatives of the state of Massachusetts, was sentenced in a federal court. He had been convicted in a US District Court of receiving a direct bribe of $65,000 for helping a software company get a state contract worth millions. More bribes for Mr. DiMasi were set to follow and, according to federal sentencing guidelines, he could have been sentenced to from 19 to 24 years in a federal prison. Before sentencing him, the US District Court Judge, Mark L Wolf, reasoned in this manner: "Which person is more dangerous to our country, someone who is doing what everyone he knows does, selling crack on a corner, or people who are undermining our democracy by successfully conspiring to sell their public office?" Judge Wolf sentenced DiMasi, who once held the second most powerful elected office in the state of Massachusetts, to eight years in prison. In 2011 the brave people of the nation of Tunisia rose up demanding democracy in mass protests and succeeded in throwing out of their country a corrupt tyrant who had been demanding for years as a matter of course bribes from corporations doing business in Tunisia. In a state with limited sovereignty, like the state of Massachusetts, democracy rules and corrupt politicians go to federal prisons. In states with full sovereignty, like Tunisia, corrupt politicians take bribes with no big cat ready to pounce on them and, when the people do succeed in throwing them out, they go into exile with their stolen money and live in luxury. The truth is that for most states in the world democracy, real democracy, can not exist successfully unless agencies exist outside of their state borders with the power to hunt for corrupt or tyrannical politicians and put them in jail for their abuses of power or for their crimes. States must limit their sovereignty and allow a central government of a worldwide union of states to watch over their democracy if they wish to live freely and use public wealth to support human goodness and universal human rights.

12

We hold these truths to be self-evident, that all men are created equal, that they are endowed by their Creator with certain unalienable rights, that among these are Life, Liberty, Property, the pursuit of Happiness, and Citizenship in a democratic state of their choosing. To secure such rights, Governments should be instituted among men with limited sovereign powers in order to prevent politicians from assuming dictatorial powers. Until the present century, independent national states required unlimited sovereignty to form national armies capable of defending states from attacks by enemy states. In the 50 united states of America, state armies are both unnecessary and illegal. In independent national sates throughout the world, national armies have become less and less necessary because the American Federal Government has assumed the responsibility of protecting foreign states from interstate wars. It backs up this responsibility at a cost of nearly 600 billion dollars a year by maintaining more than two and a half million personnel in its armed forces, military bases throughout the world, and a naval fleet present in every ocean. By joining the 50 united states as newly admitted states, national armies of new states, which sometimes are used to repress the democratic rights of their people, will become obsolete. The Federal Government of the 50 united states of North America and the Pacific Ocean has already assumed some duties of a world government partly to prevent laws and policies of national states from impeding the freedom of multinational corporations to conduct business worldwide unrestricted by national boundaries. As national states apply for admission to the American union to the Congress in Washington and are accepted by the Congress, the transition of the United States of America to the United States of the World would become gradually a reality. This extensive new world union would make more and more secure and more general the movement throughout the world of labor and capital wherever opportunities for employment draw them. The American Constitution states clearly that the Congress of the elected representatives of the 50 states possesses the power to admit new states. Since the United States began in 1787 with the acceptance of the Constitution by 3 states and in three years by 10 more, 37 new states have been admitted. The Federal Government's role as a national government would not change as long as some states in the world choose to remain independent and to retain their unlimited sovereignty. The people of newly admitted states would be citizens, as stated in the Fourteenth Amendment to the American Constitution, both of the United States and of the state where they choose to establish residence. However, as the world role of the Federal Government increases with more and more new states, its national role would decrease. This is happening already for, since the end of the Second World War, the Federal Government's world responsibilities have rendered it less and less able to concentrate on purely national goals. The limitations on sovereignty that apply to the present 50 states would also apply to new states although these limitations would tend to decrease as the number of new states increases. Who does not see that dictatorial governments scattered all over the world, ruled by politicians with rapacious designs on their own national wealth and indifferent to real democracy and to glaring world problems, must go? Limitations to national sovereignty are the necessary conditions for the establishment of genuine democracy and for the establishment of a world government capable of dealing with world problems. In the future, the central world government located in Washington in the District of Columbia will guarantee unlimited democracy to states in exchange for their acceptance of limited sovereignty and all states will be guaranteed also full democratic representation in the government of the world government.

The Federal Government in Washington has never possessed any national territory because it has been located since 1790 in the District of Columbia separated by its borders from the neighboring states of Virginia and Maryland. It has never operated with full sovereignty as have other national states since the American Constitution grants it sovereign power only in selected and limited areas. All powers not specifically granted to the executive, legislative and judicial branches of the Federal Government are reserved as areas for the exercise of state sovereignty. In fact, most Americans before the American Civil War, from 1861 to 1865, regarded the Federal Government as an agency to protect them from foreign states, to assure interstate commerce and to sort out their interstate differences and conflicts. Most regarded secession from the union as a sovereign right until the victory of the northern army over the secessionist south ended the right. The defeated general of the southern army, Robert E. Lee, publicly recognized that the war ended the right of secession but he insisted that the loss of this right meant that it was the duty of the Federal Government to use its newly-won power to assure the existence of state sovereignty. In reality, since the end of the Civil War and especially since the end of the Second World War, the Federal Government has abused and extended its powers to the detriment of state sovereignty. It has also been guilty of unjustified acts of covert and open violence against various national states mainly to secure freedom for multinational corporations to pursue worldwide economic dominance. However the usurpation of power by the Federal Government at the expense of state sovereignty has never been accompanied by the establishment of dictatorial rule in state governments. In fact, the Federal Government by law must allow the existence in the states of only democratic governments. The US government is ordered by the Constitution in Article IV section 4. to " guarantee to every state in this union a republican form of government..." Some of the present states of the union have been functioning democracies continuously since 1787 and all 50 states are now solid democracies. We the people of the 50 united states have patiently endured painful limitations to our sovereignty imposed on us by the government in Washington, but these limitations are generally those that a world union of states would need to guarantee universal human rights to the citizens of all states.

Both we the present states and any newly admitted states can not wage wars, can not set up state tariffs against free trade, can not deny residence and citizenship and the right to work and to vote to anyone, can not enact laws against the exercise of any religion, can not deprive any citizen of life, liberty or property without due process of law, can not deprive any citizen of equal protection of the laws, can not deprive any citizen of free public education and so forth. Thus, by something like a ruse of history, most acts of the Federal Government and the Federal Courts limiting state sovereignty have in reality created a firm basis in law for a world union of states by voiding state laws that might promote tyrannical powers. Moreover, the citizens of new states in the union would enjoy voting for representatives not only to their state legislature but also to the congressional legislature in Washington D.C.. In addition, they would elect a governor for their state and a federal president for Washington. We appeal to our brother states throughout the world to join our union of democratic states so that their own democratic liberties can be secured by the Federal Government's powers and so that by their presence in the union the Federal Government can assume as exclusively as possible the role of a world government which humanity needs to fulfill the good destiny that its Creator has designed for it.

More than eight hundred years ago, middle-class merchants in Europe escaped from feudal oppression by establishing themselves in towns and by guarantying their new free independent way of life with written laws. Entrepreneurs from this class made technological advances in the means of production over a long period of time that radicalized economic, social and political relations. Eventually this new middle class of merchants and lawyers created national states, first as limited monarchies and then as democracies, to protect by laws and constitutions the property and riches of the few from the working class. American foreign policy since the Second World War has continued to seek this governmental protection of the rich at the world rather than just at the national level. All revolutions are destructive but it is still possible to create a positive result of the middle-class revolution of the past if we carry its momentum further by creating a new world order that protects by law not just the worldwide freedom of the rich but the worldwide freedom of everyone. We must make an orderly transition to a new glorious condition of our world by adding states to the American union whose people will send representatives to the Congress in Washington and guarantee by the power of law both the interstate inviolability of multinational corporations and the inviolable right of the workers of the world to free interstate movement and free interstate citizenship.

We the people of the present 50 united states have national patriotic sentiments like those of people of other nations. History has taught us however that a union of states free of tyrants and corrupt politicians with a central government willing to fight anywhere in the world for the survival of freedom, as President Kennedy declared in his inaugural address of 1960, is more important than nationalistic sentiment. Two hundred and thirty-nine years ago, in 1775, the state of Massachusetts on its own put an army in its fields to fight for its independence from Britain. Independent eight years later because of help from other colonies and France, John Adams of Massachusetts refused national sovereignty for his state and instead opted for limited sovereignty and interstate union. Adams, the second President of the United States, called the men who opposed his magnanimous vision of America's future "piddling" people. No doubt people from some states, both those already united as well as those fully sovereign, will reject our vision of a future United States of the World. Some foreign states will assert that they have no need of world union with the 50 American states and other states because they already enjoy as fully sovereign states a form of world union under the protection of America. We consider their view piddling. Some people in American states, which already contain citizens of every race and religion from every nation of the globe speaking most world languages as well as English, will perhaps fear the end of the white race as a majority in America. We consider their view piddling. The world must get rid of all racism, all religious bigotry, all fanaticism, all national borders, all terrorism, all ignorance, all intolerance, all poverty, all tyrants, all corrupt politicians, all injustice or else we will all become "piddling" people and we will never have somewhere a strong central world government uniting us all under a constitution that will allow us to live magnanimously and freely in democratic states and to once again make our world green.

www.ingramcontent.com/pod-product-compliance
Lightning Source LLC
Chambersburg PA
CBHW070149290526
45789CB00002B/694